Clarinet
Solos de Concours,
1897-1980

CONSERVATOIRE NATIONAL SUPERIEUR DE MUSIQUE, PARIS

Clarinet
Solos de Concours,
1897-1980

AN ANNOTATED BIBLIOGRAPHY

Harry R. Gee

INDIANA UNIVERSITY PRESS
Bloomington

Manufactured in the United States of America

Library of Congress Cataloging in Publication Data

Gee, Harry.
    Clarinet solos de concours, 1897-1980.

    Bibliography: p.
    1. Clarinet music--Bibliography. 2. Music,
French--Bibliography. 3. Conservatoire national
supérieur de musique. I. Title.
ML128.C58G43   016.788'625   80-8360
ISBN 0-253-13577-X

Contents

Preface

In recent years, the numerous books on the
clarinet by Keith Stein, Oskar Kroll, William
Stubbins, Geoffrey Rendall, Frederick Thurston,
and Pamela Weston--to say nothing of the many doc-
toral dissertations, pamphlets, and articles by
other writers--indicate that clarinetists, both
professional and amateur, along with other performers and teachers, have had a consistent curi-
osity for more knowledge about their beloved instrument. These writings, although well done, have
yielded, for the most part, little information about
the French clarinet literature of the twentieth century and almost nothing about the famous Paris Conservatory. This institution (more accurately, the
Conservatoire National Supérieur de Musique) has
received international acclaim because of its con-
servative atmosphere, artist faculty, rigorous requirements, and competitive entrance auditions.
   Many serious clarinetists and teachers are
aware of the rich source of study and solo material
contained in many of the solos de concours. It is
certain that French composers have made important
contributions in woodwind literature and many of
them, commissioned to write clarinet solos, were
also encouraged to write for other instruments. I
hope this book will not only encourage more American clarinetists to become acquainted with some
of the solos used at the Conservatoire, but also
be a useful reference for all instrumental teachers.

Completion of this book was due to the assistance and cooperation of a number of individuals. Financial aid was received from Indiana State University in the form of two research grants during the summers of 1976 and 1977 and a sabbatical leave during the first three months of 1979. Securing many reference books on twentieth-century French music was made possible with the help of the Department of Inter-library loans of the above institution's Cunningham Memorial Library.

Recent and specialized information, not in books of musical literature, was obtained directly from musicians and agencies in France. The following generously provided information: Cultural Counselor, French Embassy in New York; Bibliothèque Nationale du Conservatoire de Musique; Messrs. Guy Deplus, Professor of Clarinet, Conservatoire National; Guy Dangain, Clarinetist, Orchestre National; Claude Gitteau, Société des Auteurs, Compositeurs et Editeurs de Musique; and Lester Warren, Edition Leduc. Mr. Warren also was helpful in forwarding questionnaires about recent clarinet compositions to younger French composers.

As editor for "Clarinet and Saxophone Topics" in The School Musician, Director and Teacher, I have been fortunate to receive many new French publications for review from Theodore Presser, sole agents for many publishers in Paris. These new releases have yielded information about the titles and composers of recent solo works for the clarinet.

Last, but not least, should be mentioned the assistance and encouragement given me by my wife, Marie Louise Gee, who, in addition to doing a large share of the typing, did the correspondence in French. Valuable and professional help in proofreading and editing was provided by Miss Mary Ellen Gee, Assistant Professor in the Arts, Communication, and Philosophy Division of the General College at the University of Minnesota.

Introduction
The Solos de Concours

The aim of this book is two-fold. First, I
hope to acquaint English-speaking clarinetists and
wind teachers with the rich source of study and
solo literature commissioned by the French Ministry
of Education for the Paris Conservatory's annual
competitive examinations from 1897 to 1980. Second,
in discussing the French clarinet literature, it is
my intent to bring out information about some of
the younger and less-known composers which, for the
most part, has not been easily accessible.

The Solo de Concours

The culmination of a student's study at the
Paris National Conservatory is the attempt to win
a Premier Prix (First Prize) within the limit of
five years' time or before reaching the maximum
age. These annual competitive examinations are an
essential part of the curriculum for all instruments. The student has one month to memorize the
required solo, which is called a "solo de concours"
or "morceau de concours," and the competition is
open to the public. The jury consists of leading
artists and the composer of the year's solo. After
qualifying in Solfège (sight-singing, while conducting), Musical Analysis and Sight-reading with
the instrument, a student is permitted to perform
in the final competition. George Wahn wrote:

Trying for the coveted First Prize and a First
Prize with Honors is a grim and serious busi-
ness because the students' future professional
careers depend largely upon the outcome. A
First Prize carries tremendous prestige in at-
taining a future orchestral position.[1]

According to Guy Deplus, newly appointed Professor
of Clarinet in 1978:

The first-year students are required to take
Solfège and Analysis in addition to the master
class for their instrument. The ideal goal is
to pass these courses at the end of the first
year in order to have more time to spend on
sight-reading and the performance requirements
on their chosen instrument.[2]

Although the musical content of the clarinet
solos varies in different years, the clarinet solo
medium has been greatly enhanced by composers who
have been invited to work in close association with
leading clarinetists. Music of composers like
Debussy, Milhaud, Tomasi, Widor, and Français has
gone beyond the very frontiers of France to enjoy
world-wide acceptance. Although the original in-
tention of the solo de concours was limited to the
diploma examinations, many of these solos have become important literature in the repertoire of the
conservatories of France as well as many schools
of music in the western world. Indeed, such names
as Bitsch, Debussy, Dutilleux, Jolivet, Milhaud,
Rabaud, and others appear on much literature studied and performed by American wind players. Edward
Burlingame Hill calls attention to Florent Schmitt's
"Introduction et Allegro" for flute and piano:

composed for a conservatory competition, [it]
far oversteps the usual limits of an occasional
piece by its imaginative charm.[3]

Many of the earlier examination solos for clarinet are well within the abilities of younger students and amateurs. While some of the solos of the
1930's and 1940's became quite technical, there
were still some playable solos, unencumbered by

technical display, chosen for these years. These
more lyric pieces, used as late as 1943, were written by such composers as Büsser, Barat, Laparra,
Dautremer, Mazellier, and Paul Pierné. Also, several of the earlier masterpieces by Gaubert, Rabaud,
d'Ollone, and Messager were brought back between
the years 1919 and 1942. However, the more recent
solos, written from the 1950's through the 1970's,
have difficult technical and musical demands and
are best reserved for university and professional
players.

1. A Brief Historical Background

Before my discussion of the commissioned solos for the clarinet competitive examinations from 1897 to 1980, it would perhaps be interesting to mention some of the early background of directors, professors of clarinet, and their pupils. The teaching, performance, and writing of these early artists developed along with the mechanical advancement of the clarinet, which led to the improvement of clarinet playing in France. In his 1963 dissertation, Joseph Caringi listed all the solos known to have been used for the <u>concours</u> from 1824 to 1960. In the historical background about the founding of the Conservatoire, he cites the earlier authors, Arthur Hervery and Pierre Constant in their writing about the foreign influences prevalent during the eighteenth century for composition, styles of singing, and instrumental performance.[1] While France was developing some remarkable wind and string virtuosi, it was Germany that was regarded as the birthplace of the early instrumental artists. Musicians were imported to perform in opera, orchestras, and military bands of the day.

Mention should be made of some of the early clarinetists who arrived in Paris to make names for themselves. According to Kroll:

The popularity of wind instrument virtuosi reached its height in the concluding decade of the eighteenth and the first two decades of the nineteenth century.[2]

4

Some of the brilliant clarinetists were Joseph Beer
(1744-1812), Giovanni Gambaro (1785-1828), Iwan
Mueller (1786-1854), and Frederic Berr (1785-1838).
All of these artists were gifted as composers and
unfortunately much of their music exists only in
national library collections. However, we should
be reminded that some of the study material has
been reprinted for the many teachers who still
find these materials useful. About the studies by
Gambaro, Pamela Weston says:

> A considerable amount of music for clarinet
> was published under the name of Gambaro by the
> family firm and by other publishers. How much
> of this is by Giovanni Battista (known in
> France as Jean-Baptiste) or how much is by
> Vincenzo (probably Giovanni's brother) is
> open to doubt.[3]

There is also confusion about opus numbers of
these compositions for clarinet. Following are
editions of the caprices reprinted by French publishers and two editions by International Music
Company of New York:

Gambaro, Vincenzo: Caprices. Lemoine, (2 vol-
    umes).
Gambaro, Vincenzo: 21 Caprices. Billaudot,
    (revision by J. Lancelot).
Gambaro, Vincenzo: 20 Caprices. Leduc 1952,
    (revision by U. Delécluse).
Gambaro, Jean-Baptiste: 10 Caprices, Opus 9.
    International, (edited by S. Drucker).
Gambaro, Jean-Baptiste: 12 Caprices, Opus 18.
    International, (edited by E. Simon).

By 1795, the French Government incorporated
two existing schools of music, the Ecole Royale
de Chant and the Garde Nationale Parisienne into
the Conservatoire de Musique. Bernard Sarrette,
a staff captain from the latter school, was appointed director of the new institution. The well-
known French composer Gossec was named as a professor of composition along with four other important names of the day--Mehul, Grétry, Lesueur, and
Cherubini--to become "Inspecteurs de l'enseigne-
ment." Since Sarrette's appointment from 1795 to

1815, directors have included the following illustrious persons:

François Perne	1816-1822
Luigi Cherubini	1822-1842
Daniel Auber	1842-1871
Ambroise Thomas	1871-1896
Théodore Dubois	1896-1905
Gabriel Fauré	1905-1920
Henri Rabaud	1920-1941
Claude Delvincourt	1941-1954
Marcel Dupré	1954-1963
Raymond Gallois Montbrun	1963-present

Early Clarinet Professors

The original faculty was organized to carry
out the duties of both instruction and performance.
Kroll states: "At the founding of the Paris Conservatoire (1795) no less than 12 clarinet teachers
were appointed who, altogether, had 104 pupils."[4]
This large group of professional clarinetists was
needed, no doubt, to fill positions in military
bands, theaters, opera and variety orchestras.
Many were also needed as replacements, as many
outstanding performers often took several months'
or years' leave to tour and give successful concerts
elsewhere in Europe. By 1808, the function of performance by the professors was completely eliminated.

Xavier and Louis Lefèvre

Xavier Lefèvre (1763-1829) was among the first
to be engaged as one of the original professors.
During his tenure at the Conservatoire, he made
many contributions to the development of both his
instrument and its literature. Geoffrey Rendall
described Lefèvre as "the greatest clarinetist in
Paris at the time."[5] During his appointment from
1795 to 1824, he had many famous pupils. Among
those who gained first prizes were Perchinier
(1802), Boufil (1805), Buteaux (1819), Crépin
(1821), and Hugot (1822). Although the records of
the Conservatoire fail to indicate the required
diploma solos from the founding through 1823 and

from 1824 to 1835, it is known that clarinet solos
and concertos by Lefèvre were used for examinations. His method, published in 1902, was probably
the most important method of the early nineteenth
century. Officially adopted by the Conservatoire,
it contained a tablature for the six-key clarinet.
Oskar Kroll reminds us that a German edition, enlarged by Hermann Bender, is still in use occasionally today.[6] Lefèvre's method, also used in Italy,
was edited and translated by Romeo Orsi and published in a revised Ricordi edition of 1939.

Although compositions by Xavier Lefèvre exist
in state libraries in Vienna, London, Paris, Berlin,
and Antwerp, the following publications of his solo
literature are available at the time of the writing
of this book:

> 4th and 6th Concertos for clarinet and orches-
>   tra, Theodore Front Music Literature 1975,
>   (score only, edited by Sherwood Dudley).
> Sonata in B$^\flat$, Opus 12, No. 1, Oxford Univ.
>   Press 1973, (edited by Georgina Dobrée).
> Sonata in B$^\flat$, Opus 12, No. 3, Siècle Musical
>   1951, (realisation by Eugène Borrell).
> Sonata in D Minor, Opus 12, No. 5, Siècle Musi-
>   cal 1949, (realisation by Renée Viollier).
> Sonata in G Minor, Opus 12, No. 7, Les Editions
>   Ouvrières 1966, (realisation by Frédéric
>   Robert). The same sonata, edited by Jacques
>   Lancelot, is also published by Billaudot.
> Six Duos Faciles, Billaudot, (edited by Lance-
>   lot).

At the retirement of Xavier in 1824, his younger
brother, Louis, was called on to become the professor of clarinet and he served in this capacity until 1833. Having had a distinguished career in
several bands, he was the first clarinetist at the
Opera from 1821 to 1824.

Frederic Berr

Next in line of the illustrious professors was
Frederic Berr, who was born in 1794 in Mannheim.
His influence on French clarinetists was profound
and it was he who helped Klosé perfect his art.

According to Rendall, "Berr held every worthwhile
appointment in Paris."[7] He also wrote much music
for military band; and in 1838, two years before
his death, he became director of the new school of
military music. His compositions also included a
tutor for the 14-key clarinet (1836) and solo works
for clarinet and bassoon. His solos for clarinet
were used for the Conservatoire in the years 1836-
1838, 1869, 1873, and 1876 and of his works, which
include two concertos, 11 solos and 28 fantaisies
on varied airs, only the following publications are
available:

> Traité Complet de la Clarinette. Leduc,
>   (revised by H. Lefebvre and P. Mimart).
> 12 Exercices dans tous les Tons. Billaudot.
> Etudes Mélodiques et Progressives. Billaudot.
> 1st Air Varié, clarinet and piano. Lemoine.
> 5th Air Varié,   "   "   "   "
> 8th Air Varié,   "   "   "   "
> 20 Petits Duos. Billaudot.

Hyacinthe Klosé

On Berr's retirement in 1838, Klosé (1808-1880)
became professor of clarinet. During his long tenure at the Conservatoire, from 1839 to 1868, he
produced many excellent pupils. One of his earliest
first-prize students of 1840 was V. Blancou, who,
besides doing valuable work on the Boehm clarinet
with Buffet-Crampon, also wrote an appendix to this
instrument for Phillipe Berr's edition of the Van-
derhagen tutor. Blancou's 40 Etudes Mélodiques
(in two volumes) are still in use. Based on the
style of Mazas, they are published by Billaudot.
Three of Klosé's famous pupils were to follow him
as professors at the Conservatoire: A. M. Leroy
(1827-1880), C. Rose (1830-1902), and C. P. Turban
(1845-1905). Other famous pupils to win first
prizes were M. P. Mimart, father of Prospère (1850),
Frédéric Selmer (1862), and Léon Grisez (1857).
Klosé composed his famous "celebrated method"
for clarinet in 1883, one year before the Klosé-
Buffet patent for the so-called "Boehm clarinet."
Kroll states:

The earlier tutors by earlier professors had to
be abandoned or re-edited. . . . An extremely
efficient revision of Klosé's tutor, in which
many well-known French clarinetists collaborated,
was published in 1933.8

Guy Dangain expresses the opinion of many that [it
is a] "veritable bible du clarinettiste."9 Klosé
composed all of the solos de concours during his
term of office. Although a few solos are still
available, most of his pieces exist only in libraries. Paul Jeanjean (1874-1928) revised a number
of these pieces for Leduc. Correspondance with the
publisher indicates no record of the opus numbers
and regretfully reports these solos to be "permanently out of print."10 Following are the study
materials and solos which are still available:

Méthode Complète. Leduc 1939 (2 volumes).
Complete Method. Boosey-Hawkes (Draper).
Celebrated Method. Carl Fischer (Bellison,
     2 vols.)
Complete Method. Ricordi (Giampieri).
Celebrated Method. Theo. Presser (Brownell,
     part I).
14 études, Opus 18. Billaudot, Leduc, Fischer
     (from works by Spohr, Mayseder, Baillot,
     and David).
6 études mélodiques. Opus 22, Billaudot,
     Fischer.
Exercices journaliers. Leduc, (revised by Paul
     Jeanjean).
45 exercices. Leduc, (revised from the method
     by Jeanjean).
Etudes caractéristiques. Leduc, (Jeanjean).
20 Characteristic Studies. Ricordi, Interna-
     tional.
30 études. Leduc, Fischer, (from Aumont).
20 études de genre et de mécanisme. Leduc,
     Ricordi.
20 études. Leduc, Fischer, (after Kreutzer and
     Fiorillo).
First Air Varié. Kalmus-Belwin.
1st Solo, Opus 9 in G. Billaudot.
4th Solo, Opus 14 in g. Billaudot.
5th Solo, Opus 15 in F. Billaudot.

7th Solo, Opus 17 in C. Billaudot.
9th Solo, Opus 25. Carl Fischer, (ed. by Lan-
    genus).
11th Solo, Opus 28 in C. Billaudot.
12th Solo, in F. Fischer, (ed. by Galley).

Lefèvre, Berr, and Klosé were not only excellent
professors, dedicated to the advancement of their
instruments, but gifted composers as well. They
wrote some 42 morceaux de concours from 1824 to
1895. After the retirement in 1868 of H. Klosé the
tradition that examination pieces had to be composed
by the professor was dropped. This change of tradition very likely occurred because more solo literature was becoming available for the clarinet. For
example, Weber's works were selected fourteen times
between 1877 and 1896. In spite of this popularity,
it is interesting to note that earlier solos by
Klosé and Berr proved so suitable that they were
chosen for use again in 1869 and various years to
as late as 1895.
The records of the Conservatoire fail to indicate the solos de concours from the founding of the
institution through the year 1823 and from 1825 to
1835. Because the Franco-Prussian War caused a
suspension of the examinations of 1871, no morceau
de concours was employed for that year. Below are
listed the examination pieces from 1824 to 1896.
An asterisk indicates solos which were used more
than once.

Year	Title	Composer	
1824	Concerto in F	Xavier Lefèvre	
1836	Eleventh Air Varié	Frederic Berr	
1837	*Third Solo, in c	"	"
1838	*Third Solo, in c	"	"
1839	*First Solo, Opus 9, in G	Hyacinthe Klosé	
1840	*Concerto	"	"
1841	*Concerto	"	"
1842	*Air Varié	"	"
1843	*Air Varié	"	"
1844	*Third Solo, Opus 1 in G	"	"
1845	Fourth Air Varié, Opus 12, in F	"	"

Year	Title	Composer
1846	*Fifth Solo, Opus 15, in F	Hyacinthe Klosé
1847	Solo Bolero	" "
1848	Third Air Varié, Opus 11, in B♭	" "
1849	*Air Varié	" "
1850	*First Solo, Opus 9, in G	" "
1851	Seventh Solo, Opus 17, in c	" "
1852	*Fifth Solo, Opus 15, in F	" "
1853	*Eighth Solo, Opus 19, in B♭	" "
1854	*Ninth Solo, Opus 25, in F	" "
1855	Fourth Solo, Opus 14, in g	" "
1856	Sixth Solo, Opus 16, in d	" "
1857	*Ninth Solo, Opus 25, in F	" "
1858	*Eighth Solo, Opus 19, in B♭	" "
1859	Fragment from Fifth Solo	" "
1860	*Tenth Solo	" "
1861	*Ninth Solo, Opus 25, in F	" "
1862	*Eleventh Solo, Opus 28, in C	" "
1863	*Tenth Solo	" "
1864	Twelfth Solo, in F	" "
1865	*Ninth Solo, Opus 25, in F	" "
1866	*Eleventh Solo, Opus 28, in C	" "
1867	*Sixth Solo, Opus 16, in d	" "
1868	*Fifth Air Varié, Opus 15, in F	" "
1869	*First Solo, in g	Frederic Berr
1870	Second Solo, in C	Hyacinthe Klosé
1872	Fourth Air Varié, Opus 12, in F	" "

Year	Title	Composer
1873	*First Solo, in g	Frederic Berr
1874	*Third Solo, Opus 13, in G	Hyacinthe Klosé
1875	*Eleventh Solo, Opus 28, in C	" "
1876	*Eleventh Solo, Opus 28, in C	" "
1877	*Concertino, Opus 26	C. M. von Weber
1878	*Concerto No. 1, Opus 73, movt. 1	" " "
1879	*Concerto No. 2, Opus 74, movt. 1	" " "
1880	*Concerto No. 2, Opus 74, movt. 3	" " "
1881	Polonaise	Hyacinthe Klosé
1882	Solo in Bb	Jules Demerssemann
1883	*Fantaisie et Rondo, Opus 34	Weber-Rose
1884	*Concerto, Opus 57, (fragments)	Louis Spohr
1885	*Ninth Solo, Opus 25, in F	Hyacinthe Klosé
1886	*Concerto No. 1, Opus 73, movt. 1	C. M. von Weber
1887	*Concertino, Opus 26	" " "
1888	*Concerto No. 2, Opus 74 (Récit. and Polonaise)	" " "
1889	*Concerto, Opus 57, (fragments)	Louis Spohr
1890	*Fantaisie et Rondo, Opus 34	Weber-Rose
1891	*Concerto No. 2, Opus 74, movt. 1	C. M. von Weber
1892	*Tenth Solo, Opus 27, in G	Hyacinthe Klosé
1893	*Concerto No. 1, Opus 73, movt. 1	C. M. von Weber
1894	*Concerto No. 2, Opus 74, movt. 1	" " "
1895	*Eleventh Solo, Opus 28, in C	Hyacinthe Klosé
1896	*Concertino, Opus 26	C. M. von Weber

Adolphe Leroy

Adolphe Leroy (1827-1880) succeeded Klosé in the professorship in 1868. During his short term, to 1876, he turned out some fine pupils, including Henri Selmer, who later won a First Prize with Cyrille Rose. From 1859 to 1865, Leroy was the director of the Buffet-Crampon company and also held positions of first clarinet with the opera and the Société des Concerts du Conservatoire. This famous orchestra, founded in 1828, under the directorship of Habeneck, gave virtually the only regular series of orchestra concerts in Paris during the first half of the nineteenth century. It was through this society that Beethoven's greatness was revealed to France. According to David Whitwell, "only Saint-Saëns, d'Indy and Gounod wrote wind music of any importance."[11] Saint-Saëns seems to have been one of the few nineteenth-century composers who had a life-long fondness for woodwind instruments. His first solo work for the clarinet was the "Tarentelle," opus 6. This work of 1851, written for flute, clarinet (in A), and strings, was dedicated to Leroy and the flutist Dorua. His "Caprice on Danish and Russian Airs," for flute, oboe, clarinet, and piano was written in 1887.

Cyrille Rose

In 1876, Leroy was given indefinite sick leave from the Conservatoire and another pupil of Klosé became professor. Cyrille Rose (1830-1903) won a first prize in 1847. He proved to be one of France's most remarkable performers and devoted teachers. As Solo Clarinetist of the Opera National Orchestra from 1857 to 1891, he was frequently consulted by such composers as Gounod and Massenet concerning technical points of writing for the clarinet. He was professor at the Conservatoire from 1876 until his retirement in 1900. During this time some of the well-known pupils to win first prizes were Prospère Mimart (1878), Salingue (1879), Henri Paradis (1880), Page (1881),

Paul Jeanjean and E. H. Stievenard (1894), J. F.
Guyot (1896), R. Verney (1898), and the famous
Louis Cahuzac (1899). Other well-known artists
schooled by Rose were Manuel and Francisco Gomez,
Henri and Alexandre Selmer. Another dedicated
teacher and performer to win a first prize in 1887
was Henri Lefebvre. Rose also collaborated with
Buffet-Crampon in experiments to establish the cor-
rect proportions of the clarinet bore.

Daniel Bonade, one of the most influential
teachers in the United States, brought out an interesting fact about the teaching of clarinet during Rose's era:

> Before Rose's time the clarinet was studied
> principally as an instrument necessary in mili-
> tary bands since there were so few positions
> available in orchestras. Rose, who was solo
> clarinetist at the Paris Opera, had a beautiful
> tone and phrased artistically and was the first
> to teach such phrasing. . . . Henri Lefebvre
> was imbued with his teacher's feeling and, pos-
> sessed of an artistic temperament coupled with
> meticulous musicianship, equalled or perhaps
> excelled Rose in phrasing.[12]

Important study material written by Rose is used
widely in both France and America and is available
in several editions. About the undisputed quality
of Rose's etudes, Keith Stein has this to say:

> The clarinet etudes of Cyrille Rose constitute
> a basic part of the clarinetist's training, and
> that repeated study of them never fails to be
> profitable. They are invaluable as a means of
> developing control and beauty of tone, and in
> instilling a sense of phrasing and melodic line
> in the student. The musical value of the Rose
> etudes is beyond question, and I find them
> extremely well-suited to the clarinet in every
> respect.[13]

The important collections of study material by C.
Rose are available in the following editions:

16 Phrasing Studies, Leblanc (ed. from 32
        Etudes by D. Bonade).

   20 grandes études (from works of Rode), Bil-
      laudot, Fischer, International (ed. S.
      Drucker).
   26 Studies (from works of Mazas and Kreutzer),
      Leduc (ed. by P. Lefebvre), Billaudot
      (revised by F. Blachet, ed. by J. Lancelot).
   32 Etudes (from F. W. Ferling, Opus 31), Fis-
      cher, Leduc (ed. by P. Lefebvre), Billaudot
      (ed. by F. Blachet), International (ed. S.
      Drucker).
   40 Etudes (from works of Dancla, Fiorillo, Gav-
      inies, Kreutzer, Mazas, Ries, and Schubert),
      2 Vols., Fischer, International (ed. Druc-
      ker), Billaudot (ed. Lancelot).

During Rose's service at the Conservatoire, a
variety of solos were chosen for the concours. In
addition to the use of Klosé's solos for four years,
it will be noticed that Weber's compositions became
very popular in 1880, 1887, 1888, 1891, and 1896.
Rose was indeed fond of the German's works and performed one of the concertos in 1862 with the Société
des Concerts. He wrote cadenzas for the two concertos and edited some fine publications of Weber's
clarinet works. Rose's version of the "Récitative
and Polonaise" from the Second Concerto was brought
back for a required solo as late as 1922 (see that
year for a list of Rose's editions of Weber). The
edited version of "Fantaisie et Rondo" (from the
Quintet for clarinet and strings) was selected for
the Conservatoire's examinations in the years 1884
and 1890.
    Sections of Spohr's Second Concerto were chosen
in 1884 and 1899, and the examination piece, "Solo
in B-flat," by Jules Demersseman, a flutist, was
selected in 1882.
    Eight of the composers of diploma solos produced
works which, apparently because of their suitability,
were used in two or more competitions. These famous
solos were by Henri Rabaud, whose "Solo de Concours"
was used five times--in 1901, 1909, 1915, 1925, and
1937. A composition by the same name by André
Messager was required for the 1899, 1907, 1918, and
1919 graduations. Other composers whose solos were
used for two or three years were Reynaldo Hahn,
Charles Lefebvre, Phillipe Gaubert, Henri Büsser,
and Max d'Ollone. Many composers commissioned to

write clarinet solos have been recipients of the
Prix de Rome, France's supreme award for musical
composition. Indeed, several of these musicians
were well known as composers of opera and important
symphonic works.

Although best known among organists for his
great addition to their repertoire, Charles Widor
wrote a great deal of instrumental music and did
much to help revive interest in it during the days
when opera seems to have had the main emphasis.
Widor and some of the other composers commissioned
to write for the Conservatoire's examinations have
been among the most distinguished musicians in
France. In addition to composing, they have been
noted organists, pianists, conductors, critics,
accompanists, and professors.

2. Influence of Opera

Historians agree that opera occupied the great interest in the eighteenth and nineteenth centuries in Paris. Although the Franco-Prussian War generated a lot of patriotic feeling toward military bands and there was much pedagogical activity at the Conservatoire during the second half of the nineteenth century, the amount of instrumental composition, especially wind music, is discouragingly small. All Music was in some measure subservient to the theater. As this tradition continued, Auber, Adam, David, and Thomas were succeeded by Gounod, Delibes, and Massenet. According to statements of a pupil:

> Massenet was not antagonistic towards instrumental composition, his great skill as a composer of opera would naturally predispose his students at the Conservatoire to follow in the same direction.1

Hill explains:

> Even if there were a preliminary test on fugue at the annual competitions for the Prix de Rome, the culminating trial was always a cantata and has remained such for the present day. . . .
> It was not until the directorship of Gabriel Fauré (1905-1920) at the Conservatoire, however, that a young composer of non-operatic tendancies was received with genuine sympathy.2

17

This composer's "Fantaisie," opus 79, for the flute concours was dedicated to the great flutist and teacher, Paul Taffanel. As Whitwell explains:

> Fauré's intent was to provide not the normal technical showpiece, but one in which the difficulties lay in musicianship. At the same time he also satirized the norm by including a few superficial difficulties.[3]

Most of the solos chosen for the examinations at the Conservatoire between 1887 and 1918 reflected the taste of the operatic and vocal composers Weber, Hahn, Messager, Mouguet, Rabaud, and Coquard. Apparently these men were well acquainted with the clarinet as a solo instrument because their examination pieces contain beautiful lyric passages with emphasis on tone quality and style. The second half of each solo traditionally stresses staccato and technical dexterity. These early solos are, perhaps, the better years for many teachers, because the composers wrote with genuine understanding of the expressive qualities of the clarinet. Many of these solos containing only two, three, or four pages, make outstanding study, contest, and recital literature for serious high school and college clarinetists.

The year 1897 marked the most significant change in the examination solos at the Conservatoire, for this was the first year in which a composer was specifically commissioned to write a solo expressly for use as a morceau de concours. From that year until the present, eighty-three competitions have taken place; each year, a clarinet solo, especially conceived, has been required. All of these solos have been written by French composers, with three exceptions. These were the use again of Weber's "Récitatif et Polonaise," edited by Rose, for 1922; "Recitativo et Airs de Ballet" by Joseph Jongen, a work originally composed for the 1941 concours at the Brussels Conservatory, in 1948; and "Reverdies," also by a Belgian composer, René Bernier, for 1960.

Charles Turban and Prospère Mimart

Charles Turban (1845-1905), mentioned earlier

as a pupil of Klosé, won the Second Prize in 1864
and the First Prize the following year. From 1868,
he was the solo clarinetist at the Théâtre du Gym-
nase, the Théâtre Italien, and the Opéra. He was
also one of the clarinetists in the Société des
Instruments à Vent, founded in 1879 by Paul Taffanel.
(The other clarinetist was Léon Grisez, whose son
Georges eventually emigrated to the United States
and performed in symphony orchestras in Philadelphia,
Minneapolis, Boston, and Baltimore.)

During the tenure of Turban as professor of
clarinet, from 1900 to 1905, his most famous pupil
was Gaston Hamelin. The Conservatory's solo competition for the graduating class of 1904 yielded
three first prizes--Hamelin, aged 20, and two others,
a year older, Georges Bineaux, and Auguste Périer.
It is rather interesting to note that the latter
became the professor of clarinet in 1919. With his
remarkable technique, rapid staccato, and a pronounced throat vibrato, his style was decidedly different from that of Hamelin, who, with others,
played in the tradition of Rose.

As a pupil of Rose, Prospère Mimart was the
first prize winner at the concours of 1878. He
performed in the Pasdeloup and Lamoureux orchestras
as well as the Opéra Comique. As stated earlier,
he also performed in the Société des Concerts du
Conservatoire. He was a distinguished soloist, and
from 1905 to 1918 was the professor of clarinet. It
has been a tradition for composers of the examination solos to dedicate their pieces to the current
professors. Mimart was very fortunate to have had
some of the greatest solos dedicated to him during
his years of tenure. The most famous of these
works, of course, was Debussy's "Première Rhapsodie,"
written for the 1910 concours. Mimart gave the
first public performance with piano on January 16,
1911; Hamelin played it with Orchestra May 3, 1919.

Mimart edited Berr's tutor and this was published in 1909. His "Méthode Nouvelle," published
in 1911 by Enoch, has gone out of print. However,
his "20 Etudes" are now available, in a version
edited by Lancelot, from the publisher Billaudot.
These etudes were completed after Mimart's retirement and were dedicated to his successor at the
Conservatoire, Auguste Périer.

Henri Lefebvre

The great tradition of clarinet teaching by
Rose gave France a legacy of master performers and
artist-teachers. Henri Casimir Lefebvre (1869-1923),
born in Lillers (in northern France), came from a
modest family background. He took up the clarinet
at an early age and later studied at the Conservatoire under the guidance of his beloved teacher and
friend, Cyrille Rose. In 1887, at the age of eight-
een, he obtained the First Prize. Daniel Bonade,
one of Lefebvre's favorite pupils, tells us:

> Rose had always considered Lefebvre his best
> and most promising pupil, and regarded him as
> his own son. When "Papa Rose" died he left his
> music and instruments to Henri. He also left
> him the mission of continuing the tradition of
> beautiful phrasing in clarinet playing that he
> had created.[4]

This tradition was continued through Henri's pupils,
who included Daniel Bonade and Gaston Hamelin. They
later came to America and did much to influence many
clarinetists in the United States. Thirty-five of
his students earned first prizes at the Conservatoire. Among them were Gaston Hamelin and Georges
Bineau (1904), Ferdinand Capelle (1905), Daniel
Bonade (1913), and Pierre Lefebvre, Henri's nephew
(1916). Bonade calls Lefebvre "the father of the
French School of Clarinet, as he had more opportunity to teach a great many more pupils than his
teacher, Rose."[5] Like his teacher, Lefebvre con-
centrated on tone and phrasing, regarding technique
as secondary. Bonade relates:

> This emphasis might lead to a neglect of tech-
> nic which, it seems, happened in the case of
> Rose. He had a beautiful staccato, but it
> wasn't very fast. The parts used at the Paris
> Opera today have many staccato passages with
> slurs marked over them in Rose's hand. . . .
> Lefebvre was the only clarinet player of his
> time who occupied, at one time or other, every
> good position available in Paris.[6]

In 1917 Lefebvre married his second wife, Marie
Louise Bonade, the sister of Daniel Bonade.

One of the finest clarinetists of the twentieth
century was Louis Cahuzac (1880-1960), who lived a
long life of eighty years. A pupil of Rose, he was
given the Second Prize in 1898 and the First Prize
in the following year. (The examination solo for
that year was Messager's "Solo de Concours.") After
many years of performing with the Opera, Théâtre
Colonne, and Concerts Symphoniques Fouché, he gave
up orchestral playing to conduct and tour as a
soloist. His tone was full and rich and pupils
came to study with him from all over the world.
Weston tells us, "He accommodated many in his house
at Luchon which was divided into apartments for
them."7

Henri Lefebvre, Cahuzac, Hamelin, and Bonade
followed in the tradition of Rose for they took
great care to play with a beautiful, round tone and
classique style. We must now turn to the composers
who were commissioned to write solos de concours
for the years 1897 to 1918.

3. Annotated Bibliography
of Solos 1897 to 1918

N.B: Degree of difficulty is based on the European classification system: 1,2,3--easy; 4,5,6--
moderately difficult; 7,8,9--difficult to very
difficult. Information marked with an asterisk
has been supplied by the publisher.

1897

Première Fantaisie
(7' 20")

GEORGES MARTY (1860-1908)
Difficulty: 5*
Paris: Leduc
U.S.A.: Southern, Geo.
  Wahr (Recital Litera-
  ture, Vol. IV)

Marty studied composition and organ with César
Franck at the Schola Cantorum and won the Grand
Prix de Rome in 1882. He was appointed as an in-
structor at the Conservatoire in 1894, and in 1903
he succeeded P. Taffanel as conductor of the famous
Société des Concerts du Conservatoire. Romain Rolland points out that this orchestra, founded in
1828 under Habeneck,

made many of the works of Beethoven and early
works of Berlioz available to the musical public. It was also at these concerts that works
by Saint-Saëns and César Franck were played
for the first time. Under the conductorship
of Marty, the orchestra, which included some of

22

the most eminent instrumentalists, began to
consider new works.1

Marty's compositions include three operas, symphonic poems, suites, songs, and piano music.
    Since the "Première Fantaisie" was the first
morceau de concours to be commissioned, it serves
as an excellent introduction to the entire catalog
of clarinet diploma solos. In Caringi's study of
these solos, he states, "The clarinet student will
find Marty's composition a recital piece of un-
usual merit, yet one which does not contain over-
whelming difficulties."2 He also quotes his
teacher, Daniel Bonade, about this work:

> French clarinetists, when performing the "Pre-
> mière Fantaisie," usually make a cut in the
> composition from measure 120 to measure 179.
> Such editing on the part of the performer may
> be excused because of the repetitive nature of
> material included.3

1898

Introduction et Rondo   CHARLES WIDOR (1844-1937)
  Opus 72 (7' 30")   Difficulty: 8
                      Paris: Heugel
                      U.S.A.: Southern, Geo.
                      Wahr (Recital Litera-
                      ture, Vol. IV)

    Charles-Marie Widor was an organist and the
first of several virtuosi on his instrument to
write a clarinet solo. A pupil of César Franck,
he succeeded him as both organist and professor at
the Conservatoire. In 1896, he became Professor
of Counterpoint, Fugue, and Composition. Although
best known among organists for his great addition
to their repertoire, he wrote a quantity of music
which included four operas, ballets, incidental
music, four symphonies, concerti, and chamber music.
    It is evident to performers that the "Intro-
duction et Rondo" is a much more difficult work
than many other solos of this period. This work,
written just one year after the death of Brahms,
seems to foreshadow later examination solos. It

presents difficult technical demands of florid and
rubato styles. The "Introduction" is a rather
brief section, serving as a preliminary to the
main "Rondo" portion. While showing certain signs
of formal design, Widor's solo does not follow
rigid structural specifications. Both the clarinet
and the piano are allowed a certain degree of tem-
poral latitude which suggests a pronounced rhap-
sodic quality. The piano opens in the first measure with a motif from the "Rondo" stated very
briefly. The remainder of the section is a free
interplay between the instruments. The "Rondo,"
according to Caringi, "shows a freedom with contrasting and related material in the episodes and
development sections."4 A coda section of 49 measures consists of rondo theme and new material.

1899

(also selected for 1907, 1918, and 1929)

Solo de Concours   ANDRE MESSAGER (1833-
   (5' 35")   1929)
   Arr. for clarinet   Difficulty: 7*
     and band: Paris: Leduc
   Leduc (rental)   U.S.A.: Southern, Kendor,
   Kendor (arr. by J.   Belwin-Mills, Geo.
     Snavely)   Wahr (Recital Litera-
                                   ture, Vol. IV)

Messager was one of the few composers of contest solos who did not study at the Conservatoire.
Instead, he had been a pupil of Fauré and Saint-
Saëns at the Ecole Niedermeyer. He was active as
a conductor at the Opéra Comique from 1898 to 1908,
at Covent Garden from 1901 to 1917, and at the
Paris Opera from 1907 to 1915. His important role
of conductor in Paris saw the premiere of Pelléas
et Mélisande, which Debussy dedicated to him. He
had immediate success with his early operettas,
given in London in 1885 and 1890. According to
Cooper:

He raised French operetta to an entirely new
musical level. . . . He worked by instinct in
a style for which his gifts were well suited.

. . . In Messager, styles of the operetta and
the opera were inextricably mingled.5

The first part of the clarinet solo presents a
joyful mood while the middle section features an
expressive melody in the low register of the solo
instrument. After a brilliant cadenza, the first
melody returns. The ending plagal cadence is, perhaps, reminiscent of the composer's early training
in modal writing.

1900

Fantaisie   AUGUSTA HOLMES (1857-
   (7' 15")   1903)
                                 Difficulty: 6*
                                 Paris: Leduc
                                 U.S.A.: Carl Fischer,
                                 Southern

The composer of the 1900 diploma solo was of
Irish parentage. She progressed very rapidly as a
child pianist and gave public concerts. Early
songs which she composed were under the pen name
of Herman Zenta. Although not a student at the
Conservatoire, she studied both clarinet and composition with Klosé. Under César Franck, she began to compose works in larger forms and aroused
considerable attention, for she was undoubtedly
one of the few professional women composers at the
time. She wrote two operas, six orchestral works,
three cantatas, piano pieces, and 117 songs, some
of which have remained in the active repertory of
French singers.

Her music, impartially considered, lacks indi-
viduality or strength; at best it represents a
conventional by-product of French Romanticism,
with an admixture of fashionable exotic ele-
ment.6

"Fantaisie" opens with a dramatic introduction
which leads to a funeral-march theme in C Minor.
The first variation, a dreamy version of the theme
in major, is followed by a second variation with
arpeggios in the clarinet part. A melodramatic

interlude introduces the third variation, which
becomes a majestic march combined with a brilliant
finale. Although somewhat dated, this work is
a convincing solo.

1901

(also selected for 1908, 1915, 1925, and 1937)

Solo de Concours   HENRI RABAUD (1873-1949)
   Opus 10 (5')   Difficulty: 6*
   Clarinet and strings   Paris: Leduc
   (out of print, avail.   U.S.A.: International,
   by rental)   Southern,
   Clarinet and Band: Belwin-Mills,
   (arr. by H. Gee)   Geo. Wahr
   Southern Music Co.

   A pupil of Gedalge and Massenet, Rabaud won
the Grand Prix de Rome in 1894. Like Gabriel Pierné, he was known as both a conductor and a professor before he became famous as a composer. In
1908, he became a conductor for the Opéra and the
Opéra Comique. From 1914 to 1918, he was Director
of the Opéra National. In 1918, he was engaged
to conduct the Boston Symphony Orchestra for one
season, succeeding Karl Muck. Following the retirement of Gabriel Fauré, Rabaud became Director
of the Conservatoire and served from 1922 to 1941.
He wrote four operas, two oratorios, two symphonies,
symphonic poems, and chamber music. His most successful opera, "Marouf" (1914), made his name famous. In this engaging work, which is brilliantly
orchestrated and enlivened with well-judged dissonances, he gave an impression of "modernity"
without altering the traditional harmonic basis of
his idiom.
   James Collis wrote about the "Solo de Concours":

   It is not difficult to understand why Rabaud's
   composition has been popular ever since it was
   composed at the turn of the century, for it is
   so entirely in the idiom of the instrument, and
   as grateful as any piece of music written for
   the clarinet.[7]

The piano begins with a three-octave pedal which provides a dramatic setting for four measures of quasi-cadenza and continues to a pedal in the dominant. The first page of this solo's exciting cadenza is, indeed, a fitting introduction to the beautiful slow movement. Although this is marked in 3/8, the feeling of a quiet, but sustained, tension should be counted in six. The allegro section in the major key is well written with motives appearing from time to time in the bass line and also developed in canonic imitation, both at the octave and in retrograde inversion. The 6/8 ending section is based on the allegro theme in diminution. The last page can be a severe test of the clarinetist's articulation. It has been a tradition in France to play a sixteenth-note G major ascending scale, beginning on the first A in bar 183 and continuing to the highest G, rather than the written notes.
Other clarinet solo material:

Etude (easy-med.). Southern Music Co.
Scherzetto (Clarinet Duet with Band). Kjos
     Music 1957 (arr. by George Waln).

                         1902

Solo de Concours   JULES MOUGUET (1867-1946)
   (5')   Difficulty: 5-6*
                          Paris: Leduc
                          U.S.A.: Southern,
                             Geo. Wahr (Recital
                             Literature, Vol. I)

Mouguet studied with Leroux and Dubois and won the Premier Prix de Rome in 1896. In 1913 he was appointed as a professor of harmony at the Conservatoire. He wrote two oratorios, three symphonic poems, chamber music, and pieces for flute, oboe, bassoon, and saxophone.
The structure of the 1902 solo is divided into two distinct sections: an andante of 52 measures and an allegro con fuoco of 85 measures. Caringi writes:

Mouguet's composition is thoroughly notated

with explicit dynamic markings. These dynamic
directives are most useful to the performer for
they leave little doubt regarding the composer's
wishes.[8]

1903

(also selected for 1920)

Sarabande et Thème Varié   REYNALDO HAHN (1874-1947)
   (6' 15")   Difficulty: 6
                           Paris: Heugel
                           U.S.A.: Southern,
                             Geo. Wahr (Recital
                             Literature, Vol. I)

Reynaldo Hahn was one of the most distinguished
pupils of Massenet. His operas and operettas were
variously successful, but he is chiefly remembered
for his songs and his settings of poems by Verlaine,
which were written in 1891-92, when he was 18. Some
of these songs have become very popular in recitals.
He was Venezuelan-Jewish by birth and came to France
at the age of three. According to Cooper:

> His incidental theatre music is in the best
> French tradition of this difficult, if subsi-
> diary, art, and his piano concerto has much of
> the unpretentious melodic charm and the drawing-
> room elegance of his master, Massenet.[9]

In 1934, he became a music critic for Le Figaro,
and in 1945, he was appointed Musical Director of
the Opéra. He wrote eight operas, three ballets,
two symphonies, a violin concerto, choruses, piano
pieces, and numerous songs.
Dedicated to Charles Turban, Professor of Clarinet, this solo of four pages is one of the most
charming of the early solos. The piece opens with
a majestic "Sarabande" in 3/2. Following is a delicate theme in 6/8, which is almost a Scottish
tune, then four variations and a short coda.

1904

Mélodie et Scherzetto,   ARTHUR COQUARD (1846-1910)

Opus 68 (4' 50")   Difficulty: 5*
                           Paris: Leduc
                           U.S.A.: Southern,
                             Carl Fischer,
                             Geo. Wahr (Recital
                             Literature, Vol. IV)

Coquart was not a regular student at the Conservatoire, but studied privately with César Franck.
He composed mainly choral and dramatic music, including five operas and an oratorio. He also completed the opera "La Jacquerie," which the composer
Edouard Lalo left unfinished at his death in 1892.

A review of an American reprint of the solo, by
Earl Boyd, calls it:

> A rather nice lyric adagio section against a
> straight chordal accompaniment, moving into
> some fairly difficult arpeggios and scale runs;
> a rapid staccato-like section, with a florid
> piano accompaniment.[10]

Caringi states the following:

> Coquard's composition displays a keen under-
> standing of the clarinet, for musical and tech-
> nical demands placed on the performer have
> obviously been tempered by the composer's thor-
> ough knowledge of the instrument. The beau-
> tiful, lyric quality of the first section and
> the lively jocular conclusion are particularly
> appealing to the student and for public perfor-
> mance.[11]

1905

(also selected for 1915 and 1916)

Fantaisie-Caprice,   CHARLES LEFEBVRE (1843-
  Opus 118 (7' 25")   1917)
  Clarinet and band: Difficulty: 5*
  (arr. W. Shepard   Paris: Leduc
  Pro Art-Belwin/   U.S.A.: Carl Fischer
  Mills)   Belwin/Mills,
                                 Southern

Awarded the Grand Prix de Rome in 1870,

Lefebvre also won prizes for chamber music in 1884
and 1891. In addition to this ensemble music, he
wrote four operas, two overtures, a symphonic poem,
and various vocal works. In 1895, he joined the
faculty of the Conservatoire.

The "Fantaisie-Caprice" is good, solid writing
and idiomatically suited for the clarinet. Because
of the length of this solo, the following cuts are
recommended: In the andante, cut one measure before
(9) and then four measures before (10); and in the
moderato, cut from (11) to (14).

Other material for clarinet:

> Andante and Allegro (Opus 102). Southern (arr.
> from the oboe solo for clarinet and piano
> or clarinet and band, by Lucien Cailliet).

1906

Morceau de Concours   PAUL VERONGE DE LA NUX
   (4' 30")   (1853-1928)
   Clarinet and harp   Difficulty: 5
                                   Paris: Enoch
                                     (out of print)
                                   U.S.A.: Geo. Wahr
                                     (Recital Literature,
                                     Vol. I)

Veronge de la Nux studied harmony, accompaniment, counterpoint, and fugue at the Conservatoire and won a First Prize for fugue in 1872. In
1874, he received the Second Prix de Rome; two years
later, he won the Premier Grand Prix de Rome for
his cantata "Judith." He wrote two operas, Lucrèce
and Zaire; some songs; and the trombone solo, "Concert Piece," which is still popular with many
teachers of that instrument. He was also a government inspector for musical instruction.

The "Morceau de Concours" is an effective salon
type, employing the combination of clarinet and harp.
The introduction in D Minor has a Hungarian flavor;
it is followed by an eight-measure technical passage for unaccompanied clarinet. The Andante theme
in D Major is separated from its two variations by
an effective 2/4 Allegro section.

1907

Solo de Concours   ANDRE MESSAGER (1833-
   (see 1899)   1929)

1908

Solo de Concours   HENRI RABAUD (1873-1949)
   Opus 10
   (see 1901)

1909

Fantaisie Appassionata   AMEDEE REUCHSEL (1875-
   (7' 20")   1931)
                                 Difficulty: 6
                                 Paris: Lemoine (out of
                                    print)

Reuchsel was a pupil of the Brussels Conservatory and studied composition with Gabriel Fauré in
Paris. He was an organist at St. Denis and won
the Prix Chartier for chamber music in 1908. He
edited the 18-book collection, Solfège Classique et
Moderne, for the Conservatoire in Paris.
   Fantaisie Appassionata has a four-page clarinet
part consisting of an eighteen-measure introduction,
marked "Lent," in the key of C Minor for the solo
instrument, and an "Allegro appassionato" in sonata
form. The beginning motive, a descending perfect
fourth, appears frequently in all parts of the solo.
A development section of 56 measures leads to D Minor and extensive chromatic modulation to the loud-
est level of the piece, marked "fff," with an ascending line to the altissimo "A" for the clarinet.
The introductory "Lent" returns briefly before a
return of the Allegro appassionato. The same development occurs again, but in the tonic key of C Major.
After a six-measure bridge section of sixteenth notes
(andante grandioso), a coda, beginning with the perfect fourth theme in augmentation, marked "allegro,"
brings the solo to an energetic conclusion.
   Reuchsel shows himself to be a master of chromatic harmony and thematic development. His later

solo written for the Brussels Conservatory (listed
below), indicates that the composer has a fine understanding of idiomatic writing for the clarinet.
His 1909 solo was probably never reprinted because
of the competition of fine solos composed by Debussy, Gaubert, Büsser, and d'Ollone in the years
following.
Other clarinet solo:

Deuxième Fantaisie. Evette & Schaeffer (dedicated to M. Bageard, Professor of the
Brussels Conservatory).

1910

Première Rhapsodie (7')   CLAUDE DEBUSSY (1862-1918)
   Clarinet and piano   Difficulty: 8
   Clarinet and   Paris: Durand
   orchestra

Like Monet in painting and Mallarmé in poetry,
Debussy created a peculiarly sensitive style in his
music, depicting half-lit delicate colors. He
makes use of whole-tone scales and oriental penta-
tonic scales. Reviving the archaic practice of
using consecutive fourths and fifths, he employed
them freely in his instrumental works. He also
anticipated dissonance so that unresolved discords
freely followed one another. In his construction,
traditional development is abandoned, and the
themes themselves are shortened and rhythmically
sharpened.
The famous "Première Rhapsodie" was originally
composed for the 1910 solo de concours. Two years
later, the composer orchestrated his piano accompaniment; this version has become one of the most
frequently performed and recorded compositions for
clarinet and orchestra. Debussy gave evidence of
an indulgent tenderness, like that of an unfavored
child, for his clarinet "Rhapsodie." In the "Rhapsodie for Saxophone," commissioned by Mrs. Elisa
Hall in 1904, we see much more original use of
oriental influence. However, history tells us that
the composer lost interest in the latter work, originally named "Rhapsodie Orientale," and it was left

unfinished at his death, to be completed by Roger
Ducasse. Kroll says of the clarinet work:

> make[s] exceedingly great demands on tone
> cultivation and production. . . . It has
> rightly been said that [this work has] advanced
> the skill of clarinettists by a considerable
> amount.12

Other clarinet solos:

Petite Pièce (1910). Durand. (originally written
    as a sight-reading test piece for the Con-
    servatoire).
Clair de Lune (arr. by G. Hamelin). Jobert.
Le Petit Nègre (arr. by A. Périer). Leduc.
1st and 2nd Arabesques (arr. by Pagout).
    Durand.
La Fille aux Cheveux de Lin (arr. Lucas).
    Durand.
Air de Lia. Edition Musicus.
Mandoline. Edition Musicus.

1911

(also selected for 1942)

Fantaisie (6' 15")   PHILIPPE GAUBERT (1879-
                                    1941)
                                Difficulty: 7-8
                                Paris: Heugel
                                U.S.A.: Carl Fisher,
                                    Southern, Geo. Wahr
                                    (Recital Literature,
                                    Vol. IV)

    A distinguished flutist and composer, Gaubert
attained the First Prize in flute in his first
attempt, at the age of 15. In 1905, he won the
Second Prix de Rome in composition. From 1919 to
1938, he was the conductor for the Conservatoire
Concerts, and in 1920, he was appointed first conductor at the Opera. In addition to a busy sche-
dule of conducting and teaching at the Conservatoire, he still found time to write two operas,
four symphonies, a ballet, an oratorio, five suites,

a violin converto, a piece for cello and orchestra,
and chamber music. He also wrote flute solos and
collaborated with his teacher, Taffanel, in writing
the famous flute method.

The "Fantaisie" for clarinet and piano is a
very effective four-page solo and shows much influence of Debussy.

Other solos used by clarinetists:

Deux Pièces (1. Romance, 2. Allegro. 6*).
Paris: Leduc (arr. from oboe pieces by Paquot).
U.S.A.: Carl Fischer.

1912

(also selected for 1919)

Pastorale, Opus 46   HENRI BÜSSER (1872-1973)
   (5' 40")   Difficulty: 6*
   Clarinet and small   Paris: Leduc[13]
   orchestra (2 hns.,   U.S.A.: International
   harp, and strs.)

Büsser was the only composer to have been commissioned to write three different solos de concours.
He studied composition under Giraud, Debussy's
teacher, and obtained the Prix de Rome in 1893; he
also studied organ with Charles Widor. He was professor of Composition at the Conservatoire from 1930
to 1948; in addition, he served for 37 years as a
conductor at the Opéra. He was a prolific composer,
having written three operas, many orchestral works,
compositions for small orchestra, and several concertos and solos for various instruments.

"Pastorale," the best of Büsser's competitive
clarinet solos, shows influence of Impressionism.
Excellently written for clarinet and piano, it has
much appeal for an audience.

Other clarinet solos:

Andante. Leduc (from Opus 22, out of print, 4*).
Aragon, Opus 91. Leduc, 1934 (6*).
Cantegril, Opus 72. Leduc, 1924 (8*).
Valse-Impromptu. Lemoine (clar. in A, arr. from
       orchestral work, Suite Brève).

Un Soir de Mai. Lemoine (arr. from A la Villa
    Medicis).

1913

(also selected for 1926 and 1941)

Fantaisie Orientale   MAX D'OLLONE (1875-1959)
    (6' 45")   Difficulty: 6*
                             Paris: Leduc
                             U.S.A.: Southern,
                                 Geo. Wahr (Recital
                                 Literature, Vol. IV)

A prolific composer, conductor, and writer on
musical subjects, Max d'Ollone won the Grand Prix
de Rome in 1897. Hill speaks of d'Ollone as an
example of "Massenet's pervading vitality as a
teacher, especially in connection with opera."[14]
D'Ollone was a professor at the Conservatoire and
was active as an opera conductor in Paris and the
French provinces. He wrote five operas, a fantaisie for piano and orchestra, chamber music, and
many songs.
    Daniel Bonade (1896-1976) won his First Prize
at the Conservatoire playing "Fantaisie Orientale"
in 1913. His edited version in Sixteen Grands Solos
de Concert (Southern) will enhance a student's understanding and performance of this solo.

1914

Cantilène et Danse   J. G. PENNEQUIN
    (6')   Difficulty: 6*
                            Paris: Leduc

Neither the Bibliothèque Nationale[15] nor the
Société des Auteurs, Compositeurs et Editeurs de
Musique[16] has any record of this composer.
    The solo consists of an expressive mood, marked
"modéré," in common time; and a faster section,
marked "assez vif," in 2/4 (quarter note = 120).
The piece presents good expressive and technical
study material for the clarinetist. The piano

accompaniment is moderate-to-difficult and contains
textures of highly chromatic writing.
   Other clarinet solo:

   Légende. Leduc (out of print, 5*).

                        1915

Solo de Concours   HENRI RABAUD (1873-1949)
   Opus 10
   (see 1901)

                 1916 and 1917

Fantaisie-Caprice   CHARLES LEFEBVRE (1843-
   Opus 118   1917)
   (see 1905)

                        1918

Solo de Concours   ANDRE MESSAGER (1833-
   (see 1899)   1929)

4. The Period between the World Wars

[F]rom 1900 to the beginning of the second
World War, France, more than any other country,
represented all that was best and most vital
in twentieth-century music. It would indeed
be no exaggeration to say that during this period French music and modern music had become
synonymous; and the period saw a rare flowering
of genius as well as of many great and varied
talents.[1]

In addition to the commissioned works for the
Conservatoire's solo de concours, many worthwhile
solo and chamber music compositions were written
for the clarinet in the first four decades of the
twentieth century. To discuss all of this literature would exceed the bounds of this book. However, such outstanding composers as Camille Saint-
Saëns (1835-1921), Gabriel Pierné (1863-1937), and
Florent Schmitt (1870-1958) cannot be ignored. The
appealing concertante-style "Sonata," Opus 167 by
C. Saint-Saëns was written in the last year of the
composer's life. It was published by Durand and
dedicated to Auguste Périer; the English artist
Jack Brymer comments:

> Not as easy as it looks, especially the finale.
> Slow movement is weak, but the second is a very
> attractive scherzo which can stand alone.[2]

Originally published by Leduc, Pierné's two pieces
"Sérénade," Opus 7 and "Canzonetta," Opus 19 are

charming and pleasant. The publication of Florent
Schmitt's "Andantino," Opus 30 bis in 1906, for
clarinet and piano, was originally an arrangement
from a vocalise. The "Sonatine," Opus 85 (1936)
for flute, clarinet (in A), and piano; the "A tour
d'anches," Opus 97 (1943); the "Chants Alizés,"
Opus 125 (1955), for quintet; and "Sextuor," Opus
129 for six clarinets, performed in 1953, show the
composer's interest in using the clarinet in a variety of ensemble settings.

Charles Koechlin (1867-1950) had a long career
which stretched over sixty years and his "diverse
musical outpourings include 230 opus numbers which
still remain largely unpublished and unperformed."3
A pupil of Fauré at the Paris Conservatory and later
a teacher of Poulenc, Tailleferre, Sauguet, and
others, Koechlin was also an esteemed critic and
theorist. During his life, he witnessed a virtual
revolution in French attitudes toward music, from
Debussy's first performance of "Prélude à l'après-
midi d'un Faune" to the atonal and serial techniques
of Schoenberg and Webern. In addition to using the
clarinet in many of his chamber and orchestral compositions, Koechlin left eight solo works for clarinet which are listed below:

Première Sonata, Opus 85, 1923.
Seconde Sonata, Opus 86, (?).
Sonatine Modale, Opus 155, 1935-36, (flute and
    clarinet).
Idylle, Opus 155 bis. Chant du Monde, 1936,
    (two clarinets).
Quatre Petites Pièces, Opus 173. Eschig, 1938,
    (clarinet and horn).
Quatorze Pièces, Opus 178, 1942, (clarinet and
    piano).
Quinze Pièces, Opus 195. Billaudot, 1943-44,
    (two clarinets, revised by Robert Fontaine,
    1978).
Sept Monadies, Opus 216. Eschig, 1948, (clarinet,
    unaccompanied).

According to Mme Li-Koechlin, the clarinet sonatas of Opus 85 and 86 were contracted for publication in 1946 by the small company, L'Oiseau Lyre.4
However, the owners died and the sonatas were never
published. Since 1970, several of Koechlin's other

compositions have been re-issued by Eschig and Salabert. It is hoped that more clarinet compositions
from this master will be available in the near future.

Paul Jeanjean (1874-1928) was a pupil of C.
Rose and received a First Prize in 1894. He was
solo clarinetist of the Garde Républicaine and was
also the first clarinetist of the classical concerts
at Monte Carlo. To Russell A. Landgrabe, solo clarinetist of the U. S. Navy Band, Daniel Bonade re-
marked:

> I have heard Jeanjean play and he was a remark-
> able artist of the clarinet--especially when he
> performed his own compositions. He has written
> some of the most beautiful music for the clari-
> net ever committed to paper.[5]

Following are his clarinet études and studies:

Vade-mecum du clarinettiste. Leduc, 1927
    (6 studies, 6-8*).
60 études progressives et mélodiques. Leduc,
    1928-29.
    Book 1: 20 Etudes (assez facile, 4-5*).
    Book 2: 20 Etudes (moyenne force, 5*).
    Book 3: 20 Etudes (assez difficile, 6*).
25 études techniques et mélodiques. Leduc.
    Book 1: 16 Studies (solo clarinet).
         8 Studies (with opt. accomp.,
          2 clarinets).
         1 Study (for two clarinets).
    Book 2: 8 Studies (2nd and 3rd clarinet
          parts).
16 études modernes. Leduc (7-8*).
18 études de perfectionnement. Billaudot.
    U.S.A.: Alfred.

Following are Jeanjean's solos for clarinet and
piano:

Second Andantino. Billaudot. Alfred.
Au clair de la lune. Billaudot. Alfred.
Clair matin. Billaudot. Alfred.
Heureux temps. Billaudot.
Rêverie de printemps. Billaudot.
Scherzo Brillante. Southern (Ed. Bonade).

Andantino. Southern (Ed. Bonade).
Carnival of Venice Variations. Salabert. Fischer.
Arabesques. Billaudot. Alfred.
Prélude et Scherzo. Leduc.

In Vinton's Dictionary of Contemporary Composers, Henri Barraud writes:

> During 1919-29 French musical life flourished
> in an extraordinary manner. The number of com-
> posers and virtuosos in Paris was quite large,
> and one could count on at least five or six
> concerts a day in the various theaters and con-
> cert halls. Publishers welcomed new music. . . .
> A new generation made a rather noisy entrance
> after 1919. The greatest amount of attention
> was accorded "Les Six." . . . All of this
> changed rather suddenly with the economic col-
> lapse of 1929. The publishing houses became
> much more cautious. The result was a lowering
> in the quality of new works selected and a grow-
> ing (and justifiable) suspicion on the part of
> audiences toward all new or unfamiliar music. .
> . . In order to give people a chance to hear
> contemporary music written for chamber ensembles,
> the most prominent French and foreign composers
> in Paris (from Milhaud and Honegger to Prokofiev
> and Martinu) founded the "Triton" association.6

Of the group, "Les Six," Darius Milhaud (1892-1974),
Arthur Honegger (1892-1955), and Francis Poulenc
(1899-1963) left a significant body of literature
for wind instruments. Milhaud's solo works will be
discussed in Chapter 7. The only composer of "Les
Six" who wrote nothing for winds was Louis Durey.
Germaine Tailleferre, born in 1892, wrote a "Sonata"
(1957) for clarinet solo (Broude edition) and "Arabesques" for clarinet with piano (Lemoine). The
latter work, written at an earlier date, was copy-
righted in 1973. A review of this work by George
Townsend follows:

> This charming two-minute work by the feminine
> representative of "Les Six" is the perfect en-
> core piece. In the key of B-flat Minor (concert),
> the composition is spiritually akin to Debussy's
> "Piece" for clarinet and piano in its regular

phrasing, rhythmic liveliness and utter lack of
pretense. Highly recommended.[7]

Georges Auric, born in 1899, wrote "Imaginées 3"
(Salabert) and a "Trio" (1938) for oboe, clarinet,
and bassoon. Other successful reed trios were written by Henri Rabaud, Jacques Ibert, Darius Milhaud,
Marcel Orban, Henri Tomasi, and Jean Rivier.
    Poulenc's first works for winds were cast in
the traditional sonata form: the "Sonata" (1918)
for two clarinets (in B-flat and A) and the "Sonata"
(1922) for clarinet and bassoon. His "Sextuor" for
piano and woodwind quintet was completed in 1939-40.
Bernac tells about the composer's three sonatas for
winds:

> In the nineteen-forties, he wrote two sonatas,
> one for violin and piano and one for cello and
> piano. But as he himself confessed, he was
> less at ease with strings, and in 1957 and 1962
> he returned to wind instruments with three so-
> natas: for flute and piano, clarinet and piano,
> and oboe and piano.[8]

    Igor Stravinsky broke new ground in 1919 with
an important work, "Three Pieces for Clarinet solo."
They were written and dedicated to Werner Reinhart,
a wealthy amateur clarinetist whose generosity made
it possible to stage the composer's ballet, "The
Soldier's Tale." In Stravinsky's famous miniature
suite, he explores some of the virtuoso qualities
of the instrument. It is a true gem in the clarinetist's recital repertoire. According to Weston:

> Louis Cahuzac made a speciality of Stravinsky's
> "Three Pieces." When he first played the pieces
> to Stravinsky, the composer found his interpre-
> tation too romantic, so Cahuzac spent consider-
> able time studying them under the composer at
> his own home in order to get them exactly as
> wanted.[9]

Cahuzac, Hamelin, and Périer

    Louis Cahuzac collaborated with many composers
and gave first performances of Honegger's "sonatine"

of 1921 and Milhaud's "Sonatine" of 1927, which
were written for him. The former composer's earliest work for winds was the "Rhapsodie" for two
flutes, clarinet, and piano (1917). His little
"Sonatine" has a particularly witty and somewhat
jazz-like last movement with a glissando, but Cahuzac did not choose to use this striking inflection
when he performed the work. Cahuzac also premiered
the "Concerto" for clarinet and strings by Jean
Rivier (born in 1896), a member of the "Triton
Group." Weston reminds us:

> Some of Cahuzac's finest work was done when he
> reached his 70's, particularly recordings of
> the Mozart "Concerto" (he had already made one
> in 1929) and the Nielsen "Concerto" in 1954. .
> . . In 1957 the Hindemith "Concerto" was re-
> corded under the composer's baton.[10]

Following are Louis Cahuzac's compositions: (N.B.:
The asterisk indicates that orchestral accompaniment
is available on rental from the publisher.)

> Arlequin. Billaudot, 1975 (clarinet, unaccom-
>   panied).
> Cantilena.
> *Fantaisie Variée sur un vieil Air Champêtre.
>   Hansen, 1972.
> Pastorale cévenole. Billaudot, 1972.
> *Variations sur un Air du Pays d'Oc. Leduc, 1953.
> Sonate classique No. 1 and No. 2. Billaudot
>   (clarinet duet, after Gebauer).

In 1922, the conductor Serge Koussevitsky began
the habit of returning to Paris for vacations and
to conduct special concerts. According to Wolff,
the maestro hired some of the elite French instrumentalists for the Boston Orchestra.[11] Gaston Hamelin, born in Saint Georges (in the Gascon region
of southwestern France), was playing many concerts
in Paris in addition to performing with the Opera.
It was not surprising that Koussevitsky invited
Hamelin to be the principal clarinet of the Boston
Symphony Orchestra. By 1932, Hamelin had returned
to Paris to play with the Concerts Colonne, and in
1943, Charles Munch invited him to become the solo
clarinetist in the newly formed Orchestre National.

He remained in this position until his death on
September 8, 1951. A consultant for the H. and
A. Selmer Company, he helped develop the "balanced
tone" model. This was the largest bore ever
used for clarinets and it certainly accounted for
Hamelin's beautiful, round tone. During his time
in the Orchestre National, one never heard a thin
sound from that clarinet section. Hamelin was
short in stature and his stubby fingers needed
little curve to manipulate the keys of his instrument brilliantly. The famous recording made by
him of the Debussy "Rhapsodie" (Victor 11433) and
his two publications for Leduc were done after his
return from Boston. His transcription of Ravel's
charming "Pièce en forme de habanera" and his excellent book, Gammes et exercices, have had wide
use. Rosario Mazzeo, a former Hamelin pupil and
retired bass clarinetist of the Boston Symphony,
had this to say about the famous book of scales,
published in 1930:

> These are extremely valuable and the student
> should not move through them too quickly. . . .
> [I]n the first form we break away from tonal
> orientation, thus acquiring a freedom which is
> absolutely essential to the mastery of the ins-
> trument--especially with today's atonal, poly-
> tonal and what-have-you-music. Though Hamelin
> starts his scales on the keynote and extends
> them over as much of the range as this allows
> from tonic to tonic, he repeats the scales on
> different fulcrums. This is critically impor-
> tant.[12]

In 1919, Gaston Hamelin was out of Paris for
military service and was not available for consider-
ation as professor of clarinet at the Conservatoire.
After World War II, I became a pupil and close
friend of this man and quickly discovered that he
was highly respected as an artist and teacher, both
internationally and in his own country. Many for-
eigners came to his home in Colombes (near Paris)
for advanced study, and many of his French students
became performers in the Garde Républicaine Band
and in French orchestras.
    To list the many dedicated clarinetists who have
performed in important orchestral posts and taught

in many parts of France would exceed the scope of
this book. However, this study of clarinet literature should include those instrumentalists who have
composed and edited well-known materials for clarinet study. Jacques Lancelot, who left important
positions in Paris in order to give more time to
solo and ensemble performances in France as well as
in other European countries, has premiered many
concertos which were dedicated to him, participated
in chamber music, and made many recordings. A dedicated teacher, he serves as Professor of Clarinet
at the Conservatoire National de Musique in Rouen.
His teacher was Fernand Blachet, professor at the
Ecole Nationale de Musique in Caen. Monsieur Lancelot has composed and edited many books of clarinet
etudes and studies as well as reprints and trans-
criptions of classics for the publishers Billaudot
and Transatlantiques.

Two other clarinetists, Ferdinand Capelle and
Eugène Gay, also wrote study materials of merit
for the clarinet. Leduc published Capelle's "20
grandes études" in two volumes; the studies were
chosen from the works of Sivori, A. Charpentier,
Rode, Fiorillo, and Vieux. Eugène Gay, who was professor of clarinet at the Conservatoire National at
Lyons, wrote a sizeable amount of educational material. His works are as follows:

> Grande Méthode. Billaudot, 1932 (in two vols.
>   of 160 pages each).
> Pratique du solfège élémentaire. Billaudot
>   (through the study of clarinet).
> 24 études pour accéder au degré supérieur.
>   Billaudot.
> 30 études de style. Billaudot (with accomp.
>   for 2nd clarinet).
> Etudes-récapitulation de technique journalière.
>   Leduc.

The clarinetist and bandmaster Henri Sarlit published "25 Virtuoso Studies after the works of Cho-
pin and Schumann" and, in 1937, a book of duets
based on old masters. Both of these books are also
available in German.

Auguste Eléonore Périer was born in Lunel in
1883 and died in 1947. He was first clarinetist at
the Opéra Comique and became an acting professor at

the Conservatoire in 1919. A year later he was
named the permanent professor of clarinet. Kroll
speaks of technique during Périer's tenure from
1919 to 1947:

> The increasingly great demands made by more
> recent composers on the fingering skill of
> players have led to the publication of many
> more volumes of exercises. In particular,
> French clarinetists and teachers concerned
> themselves with the extension of study material
> and wrote numerous considerable works. Out-
> standing among these are études by A. Périer,
> clarinet professor at the Paris Conservatoire.[13]

While some of the solos of the 1930's and '40's
became quite difficult, some playable pieces unencumbered by technical display were still chosen for
the concours. These more lyric pieces, used as
late as 1943, were written by such composers as
Golestan, Laparra, Mazellier, Dautremer, and Paul
Pierné. In addition, several of the earlier masterpieces by Gaubert, Rabaud, d'Ollone, and Messager were brought back between 1919 and 1942.
Auguste Périer recorded the following solos:

> Henri Büsser: Cantegril, Columbia D 19125
> Stan Golestan: Eglogue, Columbia DF 1241
> Henri Rabaud: Solo de Concours, Columbia D 11015

These recordings were all 78's and are out of pro-
duction, but a reissue by the Grenadilla Legacy
Series (GS-1006) contains the following:

> Jeanjean: Arabesques (Cahuzac)
> Honegger: Sonatine (Cahuzac)
> Pierné: Canzonetta (Cahuzac)
> Debussy: Première Rhapsodie (Hamelin and orch.)
> Rabaud: Solo de Concours (Périer)

Périer wrote the following books of etudes and
studies, all published by Leduc:

> Le débutant clarinettiste (1 and 2).
> 331 exercices de mécanisme.
> Etudes de genre et d'interprétation (2 vols.).
> Recueil de sonates (3 vols.).

Vol. 1: Nardini, Geminiani, Bach, Biber,
        Corelli, Vitali, Leclair
Vol. 2: Porpora, Tartini, Leclair, Gemin-
        iani, Nardini, Veracini
Vol. 3: Bach, Vivaldi, Nardini, Porpora,
        Locatelli, Geminiani

Etudes-caprices en forme de duos (after Wien-
    iawski, 5 and 6*).
30 études (6 and 7*).
22 études modernes (7 and 9*).
20 études de virtuosité (7 and 8*).
20 études faciles et progressives (3 and 4*).

5. Annotated Bibliography of Solos 1919 to 1947

1919

Pastorale, Opus 46   HENRI BÜSSER (1872-1973)
  (see 1912)

1920

Sarabande et Thème Varié   REYNALDO HAHN (1874-1947)
  (see 1901)

1921

Fantaisie Italienne   MARC DELMAS (1885-1931)
  Opus 110 (5' 35")   Difficulty: 6
                           Paris: Andrieu Frères
                           U.S.A.: Alfred Music Co.

   Delmas, a pupil of Vidal and Leroux, won the
Prix de Rome in 1919. He wrote seven operas, five
symphonic works, chamber music, two books on music,
and various pieces for piano and other instruments.
   In a dissertation about the compositional techniques employed in twentieth-century clarinet solos,
George Knight states the following about Delmas'
1921 clarinet solo:

   The effects of impressionism are seen in the
   use of parallelism and modified versions of
   whole-tone scales. For the most part, however,

the work never departs from the tonal schemes
indicated by the key signatures. The clarinet
part is quite definite in its outline of traditional harmonic progressions and diatoni-
cism. . . . Melodic contours are generally
smooth. Some passages are angular, but serve
as embellishments (see measures 3, 37, and 93-
96). While these passages are not seen as pri-
mary melodic material, they do constitute a
performance problem for the clarinetist, in-
volving, as they do, repeated leaps.[1]

Other clarinet solos:

Clair de Lune. Billaudot.
Conte Rose. Billaudot.
Soir d'été. Billaudot.
Variation Tendre. Billaudot.
Promenade. Billaudot. Rubank.

                            1922

Récit et Polonaise   CARL MARIA VON WEBER
   (Concerto No. 2,   (edited by C. Rose)
   Opus 74)   Difficulty: 7-8
   Orchestra: Breitkopf-   Paris: Billaudot
   Haertel
   Band: Boosey-Hawkes

    Since 1897, clarinet competition solos has been
especially conceived by French composers. In 1922,
however, an edited version of the "Recitative and
Polonaise" from Concerto No. 2 by Cyrille Rose was
chosen. Between 1879 and 1894, various parts of the
Weber "Concerto No. 2" were used five times.
    Because of Baermann's interpretation, the Ger-
man edition, and many printed in America, have more
ornamentation than those of Rose, Lefebvre, Lancelot,
and Delécluse, which usually show a more classic
interpretation. The following editions are by Rose
and other French artists:

Weber-Rose: Concertino, Opus 26. Leduc
     (revised by P. Lefebvre).
Weber-Rose: Fantaisie et Rondo, Opus 34.
     Leduc (revised by P. Lefebvre).

Weber-Rose: <u>Concerto</u> <u>No</u>. <u>2</u>, Opus 74. Billaudot.
Weber-Rose: <u>Variations</u>, Opus 33. Billaudot.
Weber-Rose: <u>Solo</u> <u>sur</u> <u>le</u> <u>Freishütz</u>. Leduc.
Weber-Delécluse: <u>Concerto</u> <u>No</u>. <u>1</u>, Opus 73.
    Leduc.
Weber-Delécluse: <u>Concerto</u> <u>No</u>. <u>2</u>, Opus 74.
    Leduc (cadenza by J. Ibert).

                        1923

<u>Lamento</u> <u>et</u> <u>Tarentelle</u>   GABRIEL GROVLEZ (1879-
    (4' 45")   1944)
                            Difficulty: 6 and 7*
                            Paris: Leduc

    Grovlez, one of the most gifted pupils of Fauré,
was inevitably influenced by Debussy. He also
studied with Lavignac and Gedalge and won the First
Prize in 1899 for piano. After an engagement as
conductor at the Opéra Comique and the Théâtre des
Arts, he was appointed conductor at the Paris Opera
in 1914. He also conducted the Chicago Opera Company in 1921-22 and during the 1925-26 season.

    Grovlez was perhaps too versatile and all
    around a musician to make his mark as a really
    famous composer, though here, as in other de-
    partments of his art, he lacked nothing in
    technique and general accomplishment.[2]

    His compositions include three operas, two
ballets, three symphonic poems, chamber music, and
many songs and piano pieces. The clarinet solo's
"Lamento" has long expressive phrases and the
piano furnished a background of eighth notes with
some haunting dissonances. The "Tarentelle" calls
for fast and controlled articulation from the clarinetist.
    Other clarinet solos:

    <u>Concertino</u> <u>pour</u> <u>clarinette</u> <u>et</u> <u>piano</u> (c. 1940).
        Gallet et Fils (out of print),
        George Wahr (Recital Literature, Vol. IV).

Burnet Tuthill makes the following comment about
this work:

A charming, light work in three contrasting
sections. The first part is rhythmically
tricky, the second, pleasant and sentimental,
and the third, a gay march.[3]

Sarabande et Allegro. Leduc
     (arr. from the 1929 oboe examination piece
     by U. Delécluse).

                          1924

Cantegril, Opus 72   HENRI BÜSSER (1872-1973)
   (4' 50")   Difficulty: 8*
   Clarinet and piano   Paris: Leduc
   Clarinet and orchestra
   (see 1912)

     The first section of this concert piece on airs
from Languedoc contains a 6/8 "Poco adagio" theme
in E-flat Minor followed by two florid variations
and a cadenza. The fast section in E-flat Major is
marked "Allegretto vivo" (3/8) and requires a fast,
light staccato. This theme is skillfully worked
out in a faster section, marked "Animez," with the
clarinet playing 16th notes in 2/8 against the
piano's melody in 3/8. This solo in the traditional
harmonic medium is brilliant, but quite dated in
style.

                          1925

Solo de Concours, Opus 10 HENRI RABAUD (1873-1949)
   (see 1901)

                          1926

Fantaisie Orientale   MAX D'OLLONE (1875-1959)
   (see 1913)

                          1927

Prélude Valsé et Irish   RAOUL LAPARRA (1876-1943)
   Reel   Difficulty: 6*
   (4' 40")   Paris: Leduc

A pupil of Gedalge, Massenet, and Fauré, Laparra
won the Grand Prix de Rome in 1903. He is known
mostly for the composition of five operas; La Habanera is still in the repertory in France, and has
been performed in London, Belgium, the U.S.A., and
Italy. His music is characterized by an effective
use of folkloric themes, especially those of Spanish
and Basque origins. He was killed in an air raid
during World War II in Paris.

The clarinet solo, which was later transcribed
by Marcel Mule for the saxophone, is of medium difficulty with an easy piano accompaniment. The composer has indicated that the long cadenza between
the two sections may be cut.

1928

Fantaisie-Impromptu   ARMAND BOURNONVILLE
   (5' 50")   (1890-1957)
                               Difficulty: 7
                               Paris: Billaudot

Bournonville was a professor of solfège at the
Paris Conservatory. As a student at that institution, he won a Premier Prix in piano accompaniment.

"Fantaisie-Impromptu" opens with a free section
without measure lines. This serves as an introduction to the main theme marked "Allegretto tranquillo," in 9/8 and 6/8. The texture is strongly
in the impressionist style. Although the last
thirteen measures form a spirited coda section, the
solo does not create the excitement of many of the
other solos de concours.

Bournonville wrote other solos de concours--
in 1929 for violin and in 1930 for cornet. His
little solo entitled "Danse pour Katia" is quite
charming and is often performed by flutists.

Transcription of other music:

   Danse pour Katia. Southern (arr. for Eb clar-
      inet or alto saxophone and piano by H. Gee).

1929

Solo de Concours   ANDRE MESSAGER (1833-1929)
   (see 1899)

1930

Bucolique (5' 30")   JULES MARIE LAURE MAUGUE
                               (1869-   ?)
                             Difficulty: 7
                             Paris: Editions Billaudot

    Born in Nancy, Maügué obtained a First Prize in
violin at the Conservatoire National in his native
city. His later study of harmony and composition
led him to the Conservatoire National in Paris. He
was a violinist at the Opéra and Director of the National School of Music at Cambrai.
    He wrote solos for the viola (1928), oboe (1933),
horn (1944), and bassoon (1950). The catalogue of
the Bibliothèque Nationale also lists an orchestral
suite, Hyporchèmes, published in 1922.
    The clarinet solo begins in 4/4 time with a ten-
measure introduction marked "Large." The next section is marked "Assez large" (quarter note =72).
The third section, in 2/4 "Modéré" (quarter note =
116), presents a change of mood. With the exception
of two short cadenzas and a short return to the
first theme, the "modéré" section carries the solo
to a rather dull conclusion. The harmonization is
conventional but well done. With cuts, the solo
could be a pleasant recital piece.

1931

Andante-Scherzo   PAUL PIERNE (1874-1952)
    (4' 30")   Difficulty: 7
                             Paris: Billaudot

    Paul Pierné, like his cousin, the well-known
Gabriel, was born in Metz. He studied at the Conservatoire in Paris with Lenepveu and Caussade. According to Baker, "He wrote a number of works which
were occasionally performed in Paris."[4] His larger
works include two operas, a ballet, two symphonies,
several symphonic poems, choral works, and organ and
piano pieces.
    In addition to writing the oboe solo, "Fantaisie,"
for the 1935 concours, he was commissioned to write
"Andante-Scherzo" and "Bucolique" for the clarinet
competitions of 1931 and 1940, respectively. The

former has a solo part of only three pages, but
contains nice idiomatic writing for the clarinet
and is the more interesting of the two. The piano
accompaniment, although technically modest, furnishes a fresh combination of both traditional and
impressionist textures. The motive of the descending fifth followed by an octave leap provides
the melodic idea for both the 4/4 "Andantino" and
the 6/8 "Scherzo." An exciting closing section in
3/8 contains a hint of the original motive.
     Other clarinet solo:

Bucolique (see 1940)

                          1932

Andante et Scherzo   MARCEL GENNARO (1888-   ?)
     (5')   Difficulty: 7
                             Paris: Louis Jacquot
                                (out of print)
                             U.S.A.: Geo. Wahr (re-
                                cital Literature, Vol.
                                II)

     Marcel Gennaro, a pianist, was a composition
pupil of Charles Widor and later became a professor
of harmony, fugue, and counterpoint.
     The clarinet solo opens with a slow quasi ca-
denza followed by the main theme "Andante" (2/4).
A short cadenza connects this with a spirited middle section "Vivace Scherzo" (3/8). Towards the end
of the solo, the "Andante" returns briefly for five
measures. The last ten measures present a brilliant
coda of alternating 3/8 and 2/8 meters in the "Vivace" tempo. Harmonic textures are written in a
conventional manner.

                          1933

Eglogue (4' 20")   STAN GOLESTAN (1875-1956)
                             Difficulty: 6
                             Paris: Salabert
                                (out of print)

A Rumanian by birth, Golestan settled in Paris

as a composer and music critic. He studied with
Vincent d'Indy, Albert Roussel, and Paul Dukas.
About his music, Grove says:

> His works are impregnated with the poetry and
> colour of Rumanian folklore, which gives them
> a tender and candid beauty, and he makes skill-
> ful use of folk melodies. He has been parti-
> cularly sucessful in composition of chamber
> music.5

Golestan wrote eight major works for orchestra.
     "Eglogue" begins with a dialogue for clarinet
alone, marked "Libre et lentement." This introductory section has nineteen measures; its three
phrases are punctuated by chords in the accompaniment. It is in the next two sections where the
composer really shows his Rumanian background. An
accompaniment of sixteenth notes lends a colorful
and imaginative background to a folk-like melody
marked "Allegro moderato." This nineteen-measure
passage builds in intensity to an expressive slow
section at (C). The next section, at (D), becomes
agitated and gives rise to a cadenza of four lines,
which, in turn, leads to a restatement of the "Allegro moderato" theme. Another brief return to
the expressive slow theme provides a climax before
the short ending section in E-flat major.
     Although challenging, colorful, and well-writ-
ten, this solo does not call for any particular
articulation skills from the clarinetist.

                           1934

Aragon, Opus 91   HENRI BÜSSER (1872-1973)
   (4' 30")   Difficulty: 6*
   (on popular Spanish   Paris: Leduc
     airs)
   Clarinet and Piano
   Clarinet and Orchestra
   (see 1912)

     "Aragon" begins with an "Andante espressivo"
(3/4). The fast section, an "Allegretto vivo"
(3/8), is a dance-like theme with a variation. The
work is dedicated to the composer's friend, Louis

Messaud, Professor at the National Conservatory at
Toulouse.

1935

Ballade en Ré Mineur   MAURICE LE BOUCHER
     (6' 15")   (1882-1964)
  Clarinet and Piano   Difficulty: 7
  Clarinet and Orchestra   Paris: Billaudot

    Le Boucher was a member of the composition
class of Gabriel Fauré. He won the Second Prix de
Rome en 1906 and the First Grand Prix in 1907. In
1920, he became the Director of the National Conservatory at Montpellier. His other concours pieces
were for oboe in 1932 and trumpet in 1934. He wrote
several orchestral works, incidental music to plays,
church music, chamber music, vocal music, and piano
works.
    Although the "Ballade" was used in the 1935 con-
cours for clarinet, it has been composed in 1953.
The one movement, which is rather tonal and romantic, begins with an "Adagio" (4/4), followed by an
"Allegro" (3/8). A "Moderato" middle section brings
back the opening theme and offers some contrast in
the "Allegro" section which returns and modulates
to the major key.
    Other clarinet solo:

    Fantaisie Concertante. Leduc
        (arr. from the 1932 solo for oboe and piano
        or orchestra by U. Delécluse).

1936

Fantaisie-Ballet   JULES MAZELLIER (1879-
     (5' 24")   1959)
                            Difficulty: 7*
                            Paris: Leduc
                            U.S.A.: Neil Kjos, South-
                              ern, Geo. Wahr (Recital
                              Literature, Vol. I)

    Mazellier studied with Fauré and won the Prix
de Rome in 1909. A conductor at the Opéra National

from 1918 to 1922, and a professor at the Conservatoire for twenty years, he wrote four operas, orchestral and chamber works, in addition to six concours pieces for various instruments. He wrote
four solos for the saxophone, and in 1944, Marcel
Mule transcribed the clarinet solo for the saxophone.
    "Fantaisie-Ballet" is one of the French solos
more familiar to Americans. It has an expressive
opening "Andante," very much in the impressionistic
style. The fast section is a "Scherzo" in 3/8,
which is not as difficult as it appears. The piano
accompaniment give the solo a substantial and musical background.

                        1937

Solo de Concours, Opus 10 HENRI RABAUD (1873-1949)
    (see 1901)

                        1938

Denneriana (6' 10")   ANDRE BLOCH (1873-1960)
                             Difficulty: 7
                             Paris: Edition Gras

    Bloch was born in Wisembourg in 1873, and died
in Paris in 1960. He studied with Guiraud and Massenet and won the Grand Prix de Rome in 1893. One
of his most successful major compositions was the
Suite Palestinienne for cello and orchestra. He
wrote two works for saxophone and piano in 1932 and
1953. The following quotation about his writing is
by Vuillermoz:

    A. B. possesses a supple and refined talent
    which finds, in a classic language, all the re-
    sources necessary to treat the most varied sub-
    jects.[6]

The clarinet solo opens with a recitative which
may be cut to four measures as indicated by the
composer. The "Adagio" section in 3/4 which follows,
has an expressive melody with a good modal background of interesting rhythmic design. Pages two
and three of the clarinet part contain various short

allegro sections which are agreeable, but do not
show a great deal of musical development.

1939

Solo de Concours   JOSEPH-EDOUARD BARAT
   (5' 25")   (1882-1963)
                           Difficulty: 7*
                           Paris: Leduc
                           U.S.A.: Geo. Wahr (Recital
                              Literature, Vol. IV)

   Barat studied with P. Vidal and E. Pessard. He
was a bandmaster and founder and director of l'Ecole
Préparatoire de Sous-Chefs de Musique Militaire.
   He has written numerous solos for various instruments, and his textures are all in the traditional idiom.
   Other clarinet solos:

   Chant Slave. Leduc (band accompaniment, 4*).
      Geo. Wahr (Recital Lit., Vol. II).
   Fantaisie Romantique. Leduc (7*).
   Pièce en sol mineur. Leduc (dedicated to Ferdi-
      nand Capelle, 6*).
   Piece in G Minor. Kendor (band accompaniment
      arr. by N. Heim, 5').

1940

Bucolique   PAUL PIERNE (1874-1952)
   (see 1931)   Difficulty: 7
                          Paris: Billaudot

   Although the "Bucolique" has some nice melodic
and harmonic moments, it is too long for what it
has to say. Also, the solo does not present much
opportunity for the study of staccato or articulated
patterns.

1941

Fantaisie-Orientale   MAX D'OLLONE (1875-1959)
   (see 1913)

1942

Fantaisie   PHILIPPE GAUBERT (1879-
   (see 1911)   1941)

1943

Récit et Impromptu   MARCEL DAUTREMER (1906-)
   (6' 10")   Difficulty: 7*
   (from Page d'Exil)   Paris: Leduc

   Dautremer studied composition with Paul Dukas
and Olivier Messiaen and conducting with Philippe
Gaubert. In 1946, he was appointed Director of the
National Conservatory at Nancy and served there
also as conductor until 1969. He has written several orchestral works and solos for wind instruments. His instrumental style is well adapted to
each woodwind. The form of his music shows clarity,
and his textures are traditional and polytonal.
   In the 1943 diploma solo, a nice first half is
followed by a long and ineffective cadenza and an
"Allegro moderato."
   Other clarinet solos:

   Gavottina. Lemoine, 1969.
   Page en Contraste. Lemoine, 1971.
   Premier Souffle. Lemoine.

1944

Récitatif et Thème Varié GASTON LITAIZE (1909-)
   (7' 30")   Difficulty: 7*
                                   Paris: Leduc

   Blind from infancy, Gaston Litaize studied at
the National Institute for the Blind and the Conservatoire, later winning the Second Prix de Rome. He
has become one of France's greatest organists and
made his first American concert tour in 1957. Having composed several important church and organ
works, he shows great understanding for an expan-
sive musical construction. Claude Rostand says:

   His orientation. . .is not so much the exploitation of classical forms as it is toward the enrichment of his language. This results in a novel treatment of themes in ancient modes.[7]

His clarinet solo consists of a long recitative, followed by a theme of modal and folkloric quality, and five variations. A varied harmonic treatment supports brilliant variations challenging the agility of the clarinetist. True to the tradition of great French organists, the "Variation Finale" is an exciting four-part fugue.

1945

Préambule et Scherzo   HENRI MARTELLI (1899-   )
   Opus 60 (7' 20")   Difficulty: 8
                              Paris: Billaudot

Henri Martelli, who was born in Corsica, was a pupil of Mouguet, Caussade, and Widor. "In his compositions, he attempted to recreate the spirit of old French music in terms of modern counterpoint."[8] Of Martelli's music, Goldberg says:

In his numerous compositions M. appears as a virtuoso of contrapuntal writing, with a taste, uncommon in out-and-out polyphonists, for briskness and gaiety, for every form of divertimento. . . . This music is perfect in its somewhat restricted domain: stylized without less of spontaneity . . . it displays the pleasant stiffness of masks and is never devoid of a sort of dry Florentine charm.[9]

He wrote one opera, six orchestral works, and chamber music. The latter includes a Suite for four clarinets (1936), a Trio, Opus 45 (1938), a wind octet (1941), string quartets and quintets, as well as sonatas for violin, bassoon, flute, and trumpet.

His clarinet solo has a short and expressive "Lento," followed by a long "Scherzo" in 5/8. Although the work is well constructed and rythmic in interest, it exhibits a certain dryness and intellectualism which does not easily hold the interest of either the performer or the audience.

1946

Concertstück (6')   RAYMOND GALLOIS-MONTBRUN
                                    (1918-   )
                               Difficulty: 8*
                               Paris: Leduc

   A pupil of Henri Büsser and Jean and Noël Gallon, Gallois-Montbrun won the Grand Prix de Rome in
1944. A violinist and composer, he has been, since
1965, the Director of the Conservatoire National Supérieur de Musique. About his writing, Londeix
quotes two French writers:

   His writing is both light and solid, moving
   and subtle.10
   More a draftsman than a colorist, he writes a
   music of very fine poetic sensibility without
   affectation.11

   "Concertstück" begins with a clarinet cadenza
of five lines which includes a hint of the thematic
material later to appear in the piano part ("Andante, très calme"). At (C) a second theme builds
to a section marked "Vif" (quarter note =108-112).
This section, at (D), alternates from 2/4 to 3/4;
the mood is playful, with articulations and sixteenth-note triplet figures. A short bridge section at (E) leads to a "Poco piu lento" in cut time
(half-note =100). At (K) the first "Vif" tempo returns, and a coda section (L) increases the tempo
to "Poco piu vivo" in 2/4 (quarter note =120). The
composer has clearly marked all tempo changes and
expressive details, and while the work is difficult
for both clarinet and piano, the highly chromatic
progressions give a lush atmospheric mood and the
work is musically very worthwhile.
   Other clarinet compositions:

Humoresque. Leduc (4-5*).
6 Pièces Musicales d'Etudes. Leduc, 1955 (5-6*).
     1. Prélude (Le mouvement conjoint et rapide)
     2. Divertissement (Les Arpèges)
     3. Grave (La Sonorité)
     4. Burlesque (Staccato)
     5. Sicilienne (La Souplesse)
     6. Finale (Les Batteries)

1947

Humoresque (6' 30")   MARCEL MIROUZE (1906-57)
  Clarinet and piano   Difficulty: 7*
  Clarinet and orchestra Paris: Leduc
  (orch. parts out of
  print)

Mirouze, a composer of great talent, studied
with Henri Büsser at the Conservatoire. He directed
the Paris Radio Orchestra (1935-40) and conducted
in Monte Carlo (1940-43). He died in an automobile
accident in 1957. He wrote one opera (1952), two
ballets, two symphonies, two other orchestral works,
a piano concerto, film music, piano pieces, and songs.
Of interest to wind players is his "Pièce en Septuor"
(1933) for woodwind quintet, trumpet, and piano
(Leduc).

His "Humoresque," dedicated to Maurice Cayol, is
an enjoyable solo for performers and audience alike.
A mysterious and melancolic introduction of 18 measures leads to a short lyrical section which reap-
pears later. The main part of the composition is an
"Allegro con fantasia"; this is highly spirited and
slightly dissonant writing with a few meter changes.

6. After World War II

Creativity in France was not slowed by the events of World War II; the rationing of gas, electricity, and other items made for close contact between music and the public during the occupation of Paris, where a brilliant musical life flourished, although, for propaganda purposes, it was understandably more German than French. Paul Dukas (1865-1935) left only ten compositions, but they were all good; Baker calls him "a composer of solid attainments whose talent showed to the greatest advantage in the larger forms, which he handled with mastery."[1] As a teacher at the Conservatoire he had great influence on his pupils, and his Ariane et Barbe-Bleue is one of the finest French operas in the impressionist style. During the period of occupation, the Germans restricted the performance of this opera and other compositions by Dukas. After the liberation of Paris in 1944, much musical activity began to revolve around the Radiodiffusion Française, which had Henri Baraud, another composer, as its Musical Director until 1965. Six orchestras in the provinces were subsidized by the government and, by way of further decentralization since the war, several musical festivals have also been established in the provinces.

Olivier Messiaen

Since the beginning of the century and the striking genius of Claude Debussy, there has probably been no other influence as strong in French

music as the teaching and creative work of Olivier
Messiaen. Born in 1908 at Avignon and entering the
Conservatory at the age of eleven, he graduated with
the highest honors after completing courses with
Jean and Noël Gallon (Harmony, Counterpoint, and
Fugue), Marcel Dupré (Organ), and Paul Dukas (Composition). After leaving the Conservatoire in 1931,
he had a variety of positions, which included organ
and teaching posts at the Ecole Normale and the
Schola Cantorum. In 1936, he became active with
three other composers in a group which called themselves "La Jeune France." The members of the group,
Yves Baudrier (the prime mover), Daniel Lesure, and
André Jolivet, were a mixture of systematic progres-
sivism which permitted neither limitation nor regi-
mentation. Rostand points out:

> The group was far from enshrining itself in an
> ivory tower; on the contrary, at each of its
> concerts, it welcomed a musician who did not be-
> long, particularly Germaine Tailleferre, Claude
> Arrieu, Marcel Delannoy, Georges Migot, Tony
> Aubin, Henri Martelli, Jean Françaix, etc.[2]

Some of these composers, commissioned to write conservatory examination solos for clarinet, will be
discussed later.
     When the war came in 1939, Messiaen was mobi-
lized, and taken prisoner the following year. According to Myers:

> This was, in some respects, a turning point in
> his career, for it was during his captivity in
> Stalag 8 A in Silesia that he composed one of
> the most significant and important works--the
> "Quatuor pour la fin du Temps" for violin, clar-
> inet, cello, and piano.[3]

This full-length work of eight movements, published
by Durand in 1942, is without a doubt the greatest
piece of chamber music for the clarinet written in
this century. In the cold, mud, and snow of the
Silesian camp he wrote, without a piano, all eight
movements of this spiritually conceived work. The
third movement, "Abime des oiseaux" (Abyss of the
Birds), is written for unaccompanied clarinet, and
it can stand by itself in a recital. The following

is translated from the composer's description of
this two-page section:

> The Abyss: it is time, with its sadness, its
> lassitude. The birds make contrast: they sym-
> bolize our desire for light, stars, rainbows,
> and delightful vocalization. At the beginning:
> sadness. Notice the immense holds of swollen
> sounds (pianissimo, crescendo molto, to the
> loudest possible dynamic level). The songs of
> the birds are written in a fantastic and gay
> style of the black mockingbird. The return to
> the desolation is made with the beautiful dark
> timbre of the chalumeau register of the clari-
> net. The conclusion is on an arpeggio of the
> dominant chord which is often heard during the
> work.[4]

In 1942, Messiaen was named Professor of Harmony at the Conservatoire; five years later the
Conservatory's audacious director, Claude Delvin-
court, created for him a class in analysis, esthetics, and rhythm. Golea comments:

> [the class] was in reality nothing less than a
> camouflaged class in composition. This camou-
> flage was necessary, for to have openly named
> Messiaen professor of composition would have
> caused an insurrection in official musical
> circles. Actually for the past twenty years,
> Messiaen has been the only professor at the
> Paris Conservatory to inspire numerous composers
> and to contribute heavily to the creation of the
> decisive current in contemporary music.[5]

Messiaen introduced his students to works of Schoenberg, Berg, Stravinsky, and Debussy, and did not
limit himself to a particular school or technique
of writing. A seeker more than a head of a musical
movement, Messiaen has had an enormous influence on
a whole generation of musicians through his teaching
at the Conservatoire and through the impact of his
works.

André Jolivet

Jolivet (1905-1974) has made a substantial con-

tribution to the solo literature for woodwinds instruments. Since 1945, his works have been numerous
and significant enough to assign him an exceptional
place alongside those having extremist tendencies.
He has remained in essence the modal composer and
has, perhaps even more than Messiaen, pressed the
exploration of modes to the limit and included them
in his music. His modal language and rhythmic writing (often without bar lines) and his use of color
respond to a deep need to preserve for music its
essential role of mystic incantation. Golea states,
"Alongside Messiaen, to whom he owes a great deal,
André Jolivet represents and incarnates one of the
strongest creative forces of contemporary music."[6]
     He has written five works for flute and piano,
three pieces for unaccompanied flute, a sixteen-
minute work for flute and percussion, two works for
oboe, and one each for the bassoon and the saxophone.
In 1953, he wrote a small piece for clarinet and
piano entitled "Méditation" (Pierre Noël, Paris,
later assigned to International) and "Sonatine for
Flute and Clarinet" (Boosey-Hawkes). In 1967, an
important work for unaccompanied clarinet, entitled
"Ascèses" (Aspiration to the Higher Virtues), was
published by Billaudot. The composer indicates that
the work may be performed on either the B-flat or
the A clarinet, and he has also written an alternate
version for flute or alto flute in G. This fifteen-
minute work, in five movements, is like the work of
Messiaen in that each movement has a quotation of
some spiritual aspiration. The work has metronome
but very few bar lines. There are rhythmic and
technical complexities, but these challenges stand
as an important contribution to the repertoire for
unaccompanied clarinet.
     In addition to the two works by Messiaen and
Jolivet discussed above, other works for clarinet
solo are listed under the appropriate composers in
the next chapter. The following composers have also
contributed works for this medium from 1930 to the
present:

     Arma, Paul: Petite Suite. Lemoine, 1930
          (6' 30").
          : Trois Mobiles. Choudens, 1971 (6').
          : Rubato, 1977 (7' 20").
     Ballif, Claude: Solfeggietto No. 5. Transat-
          lantiques, 1974.

Boulez, Pierre: <u>Domaines</u>. Universal (also with
    orchestra).
Charpentier, Jacques: <u>Antienne</u>. Leduc, 1978 (6').
Constant, Marius: <u>For Clarinet</u>. Salabert, 1955
    (for Guy Deplus).
Desportes, Yvonne: <u>La Naissance d'un Papillon</u>.
    Billaudot, 1975 (to Guy Dangain, 15').
Komives, Janos: <u>Flammes</u>. Jobert, 1975 (to Guy
    Deplus).
Lemeland, Aubert: <u>Cinq Pièces</u>, Opus 20. Billau-
    dot, 1974 (to Robert Fontaine, 8' 20").
    ____: <u>Cinq Nouvelles Pièces</u>, Opus 62. Billau-
    dot, 1978 (to James Gillespie, 8').
Miluccio, Giancomo: <u>Rhapsodie</u>. Leduc, 1979 (to
    Jean Leduc, 5').
Rieunier, Jean-Paul: <u>Antienne</u>. Leduc, 1978
    (may be performed by flute and clarinet
    or by clarinet alone).
Rivier, Jean: <u>Les Trois</u> "S". Transatlantiques,
    1974 (I, <u>Sillages</u>, to J. Lancelot; II,
    <u>Soliloque</u>, to Guy Dangain; III, <u>Serpentines</u>,
    to Guy Deplus).
Robert, Lucie: <u>Dialogue avec Soi-même</u>. Billau-
    dot, 1979 (to Guy Dangain).
Tailleferre, Germaine: <u>Sonate</u>. Peters, 1957
    (for Henri Dionet, 4' 25").
Taranu, Cornel: <u>Improvisation</u>. Leduc, 1977 (3').
Tiêt, Tôn-Thât: <u>Bao La</u>. Transatlantiques, 1979
    (dedicated to and edited by Robert Fontaine
    in 1978, 11').
Tisné, Antoine: <u>Invocations pour Ellora</u>.
    Billaudot.
    ____: <u>Manhattan Song</u>. Peer Musikverlag, 1977.

After World War II, the Conservatory's diploma
solos became quite intricate and made more strenuous
technical demands. Of these solos, Caringi expresses this opinion:

The extreme difficulties encountered in the more
contemporary clarinet contest solos may, of
course, be attributed to the simple fact that
standards of performance are consistently being
raised. But a more subtle reason may account,
in part, for the complex and demanding characteristics of the recent competition pieces for
clarinet. The French school of clarinet playing,

which formerly stressed beautiful tone and
phrasing, has now placed its emphasis on the
more mechanical aspects or performance.[7]

After visiting the 1954 Concours du Conservatoire,
the American clarinetist David Weber wrote:

The younger players seem to concentrate entirely
on technique and smaller tones liberally gar-
nished with a rapid throat vibrato. This school
of playing appears to have originated chiefly
with Périer, whose studies are well known in
this country. Delécluse is the foremost player
of this style today in Paris, and his pupils
quite naturally play the same way. The other
camp is typified by Louis Cahuzac and a number
of older players. Beautiful phrasing and quality of tone are chief characteristics of this
school. There are, of course, younger players
who also play in this style; chief among them
is Jacques Lancelot, who has established a re-
putation as a soloist throughout France and
Europe. . . . It seemed to me that almost
every middle-aged or older player of consequence
in France had at one time or other studied with
either Cahuzac or the late Gaston Hamelin.[8]

Concertos and Sonatas

With this emphasis on greater length and difficulty, it is only natural that composers began to
think of larger forms, and we see in the last thirty
years an increased number of concertos for clarinet
and orchestra. Before discussing the solos de concours from 1948 to 1980, I would like to mention
some of the concertos for clarinet and orchestra,
strings, or piano reduction as well as some clarinet
sonatas which have not been commissioned for the
Conservatoire examinations. These compositions
include music written by both native French composers
and musicians born in other countries who have settled more or less permanently in France. The latter group have combined music from their national
heritage and newly assimilated techniques gained in
France into a current twentieth-century French style.
These composers are Laszo Lajtha and Paul Arma (Hung-

ary); Stan Golestan, Marius Constant, and Marcel
Miholovici (Rumania); Bohuslav Martinu (Czechoslo-
vakia); and Alexandre Tansman and Stanislaw Skrowaczewski (Poland). In addition to the composers discussed in the next chapter, the following have contributed concertos from 1940 to the present:

Arma, Paul (1905-   ): Divertimento de Concert
   No. 6. Lemoine, 1960 (clarinet and strings
   with xylophone, 12' 30").
Ballif, Claude: Ivre-moi-immobile. Transatlantiques (clarinet and small orchestra
   or piano, 17').
Beugniot, Jean-Pierre (1935-   ): Concertino.
   Transatlantiques, 1965 (clarinet and strings
   or piano, 14').
Calmel, Roger (1921-   ): Concerto. Transatlantiques, 1973 (clarinet and chamber
   orchestra or piano).
Casanova, André (1919-   ): Ballade, 1955
   (clarinet in A, strings, harp, celeste and
   percussion, dedicated to Pierre Capdevielle,
   20').
Chaynes, Charles: Concerto. Leduc, 1979 (clarinet with chamber orchestra or piano, commissioned for the Concours International du
   Festival de Musique de Toulon (18').
Gagnebin, Ruth (1921-   ): Andante et Allegro.
   Leduc, 1950 (dedicated to Louis Cahuzac
   and commissioned for the Concours International de Genève; clarinet and orchestra
   or piano).
Lemeland, Aubert (1932-   ): Improvisations
   Concertantes (with string orchestra, 13').
Milhaud, Darius (1892-1974): Concerto. Elkan
   Vogel, 1941 (dedicated to, but not performed
   by, Benny Goodman).
Philiba, Nicole (1937-   ): Concerto da Camera.
   Billaudot (clarinet and strings or piano;
   dedicated to J. Lancelot).
Rivier, Jean (1895-   ): Concerto. Transatlantiques, 1959 (dedicated to Paul Sacher,
   17' 20").
Skrowaczewski, Stanislaw (1920-   ): Ricercari
   Notturni, European American Music Corp.,
   1977 (for clarinet and bass clarinet or
   soprano, alto, and baritone saxophones and
   orchestra with one soloist, 25' 43").

Tansman, Alexandre (1897-   ): <u>Concerto</u>.
    Editions Françaises, 1950 (dedicated to
    Louis Cahuzac, 15').

Sonatas for clarinet and piano written in the
last sixty years range from the rather vague and
wandering contributions of Ludovicus Mirandolle,
who also wrote "Trois Duos" for clarinets in B-flat
and A (Leduc, 1938) to the audacious and witty sonatines of Bohuslav Martinu and Pierre Gabaye (published in 1957 and 1959 respectively, also by Leduc).
It is noteworthy that a small number of French composers seldom write clarinet solo literature in the
traditional forms--sonata, fugue, canon, or any
other ready-made mold. Following is a list of these
smaller forms with piano:

Arma, Paul (1905-   ): <u>Divertimento</u> No. 6.
    Lemoine, 1956 (13').
Beugniot, Jean-Pierre: <u>Sonate</u>, 1969-70 (pour
    la Présence de l'Homme).
Cartan, Jean (1906-1932): <u>Sonatine</u>. Heugel, 1931
    (flute and clarinet, for the International
    Festival for Contemporary Music, and dedi-
    cated to René LeRoy).
Casterède, Jacques (1926-   ): <u>Sonata</u>. Leduc,
    1956 (to Désiré Dondeyne, 13' 30").
Depelsenaire, J. M.: <u>Sonatine</u>. Gallet et fils,
    1958 (for clarinet or alto saxophone).
Gabaye, Pierre (1930-   ): <u>Sonatine</u>. Leduc,
    1959 (12').
Honegger, Arthur (1892-1955): <u>Sonatine</u>. Salabert,
    1922 (to Werner Reinhart, 4').
Ladmirault, Paul (1877-1944): <u>Sonate</u>. Leduc,
    1949 (to Victor Groff).
Martinon, Jean (1910-   ): <u>Sonatine</u>. Billaudot,
    1935 (6' 21").
Milhaud, Darius (1892-1974): <u>Sonatine</u>. Durand,
    1927 (to Louis Cahuzac, 9' 26").
Mirandole, Ludovicus (1904-   ): <u>Sonata</u>.
    Leduc, 1938.
    : <u>Sonatine</u>. Leduc, 1940.
Poulenc, Francis (1899-1963): <u>Sonata</u>. Chester,
    1962 (to the memory of Arthur Honegger, 13').
Saint-saëns, Camille (1835-1921): <u>Sonata</u>, Opus
    167. Durand, 1921 (to A. Périer, 11' 26").
Sauguet, Henri (1901)   ): <u>Sonatine</u> en deux
    chants et un intermède. Billaudot, 1972 (17').

Pieces for Students

Although the major French music publishers are
known for their releases of difficult morceaux de
concours, efforts have been made also to publish
good original wind literature for the younger student with more modest technical abilities. For
these developing clarinetists, Guy Dangain and Jacques Lancelot have each directed a series of study
and solo collections for the publisher Billaudot.
Perusal of the catalogs of Leduc, Durand, and Editions Transatlantiques will also yield a number of
well-written easier materials. Two organizations
which have encouraged composers to write original
material are the Confédération Musicale de France
and the Fédération Nationale des Unions de Conser-
vatoires Municipaux de Musique. These organizations
have sponsored competitions for composers and have
made publication possible for worthwhile materials.
Some of the composers having winning compositions
published by Billaudot are Jean-Pierre Bounty, Jean
Meyer, O. Garenlaub, René Mignion, Serge Lancen, and
W. Van Dorsselaer. André Ameller and Charles Jay
are composers published by Lemoine. Alphonse Leduc
has released a number of easy and medium works for
the more sophisticated student. Some of these outstanding pieces have been composed by Alain Weber,
a 1952 Prix de Rome winner ("Andantino" and "Mélo-
pée"); Henri Vachey ("Elégy et Danse"); and earlier
works by Barat, Clérisse, and Tomasi. Other idiomatic solos of medium difficulty from various publishers can be found from the pens of de Coriolis,
Merlet, Pascal, and Rueff.

Ulysse Delécluse

In 1948, Ulysse Delécluse succeeded Auguste
Périer as Professor of Clarinet at the Conservatoire.
Born in 1907, he won a First Prize in 1925. Active
as a soloist in chamber music and with the Garde
Républicaine Band, he was elected by a large major-
ity of votes to this post and served until 1978. He
was the tester for clarinets at the Selmer Company
and preferred the Center Tone Model, the Nine Series,
and finally the Nine Star Series. He believed these
larger-bore clarinets would help produce a roundness
of tone. In later years, the Selmer Ten Series,

a smaller bore, was developed for the American mar-
ket, but Delécluse never recommended this model.
Since 1978, one of his outstanding students, Guy
Dangain, has served as tester for Selmer. Mr. Dangain, however, performs on the Series Ten clarinet
and has helped develop an improved mouthpiece manufactured by H. A. Selmer. Born in 1935, Dangain
first studied with M. Hannert in Lille; he won the
First Prize in Clarinet in 1953, and First Prize in
Chamber Music in 1956, at the Conservatoire National
Supérieur. A principal clarinetist with the Orchestre National since 1963, he has been active in
editing the following educational works for Billaudot:

> L'A. B. C. du Jeune Clarinetiste (2 volumes).
> Cahier de gammes.
> À la Manière de... (5 pieces by Jeanine Rueff in
>   the style de Couperin, Rameau, Haydn, Cle-
>   mento and Schumann).
> Pages de style en forme de Pièces de concours
>   (works by Rueff, Pascal, Damase, Desportes,
>   Gotkovsky, and Dubois).

Another of Delécluse's more prominent pupils was
Henri Druard, who won a first prize in 1951. After
serving as Solo Clarinetist with the Garde Républicaine Band, he became Principal Clarinetist with the
Orchestre de Paris. His compositions, addressed to
the contemporary needs of the advanced clarinet players, are the following:

> 11 Modern Studies. Leblanc.
> Evolutions. Leduc, 1978 (7-8*).

Some of the other outstanding first prize stu-
dents from Professor Delécluse's classes have been
Messrs. Edmond and Pierre Boulanger, Michel Arrignon,
Serge Dangain, Michel Portal, and Miss Edwige Caquet.
Nestor Koval, Professor of Clarinet at Duquesne Uni-
versity, gained a Second Prize in 1951, and a First
Prize the following year. Two American saxophonists
have won first prize honors on their instrument:
Frederick Hemke (1956, with Marcel Mule) and Rita
Knuesel (1977, with Daniel Deffayet).
In addition to various revisions of solos, men-
tioned earlier, Delécluse wrote and edited the fol-
lowing books of etudes and studies, all published
by Leduc:

Bach: 15 Etudes (adapted for clarinet, 8*).
_____ : 6 suites (adapted for clarinet from the
    cello works, BWV 1007-12, 8*).
14 grandes études (sur des motifs d'oeuvres
    classiques et modernes, 8*).
20 études faciles (after Samie, 3-4*).
Gambaro: 20 caprices (6*).

7. Annotated Bibliography of Solos 1948 to 1980

1948

Recitativo et Airs de
   Ballet, Opus 115 (8')

JOSEPH JONGEN (1873-1953)
Difficulty: 8
Brussels: Gervan Edition

Studying at the Liège Conservatory, Jongen won the Belgian Grand Prix de Rome in 1897. During World War I, he lived in England, giving numerous chamber music concerts and organ recitals. In 1919, he was appointed Professor at the Brussels Conservatory; and he served as the Director of that institution from 1925 to 1939. A prolific composer, he wrote in all forms; his compositions include 137 opus numbers. Since he lived at the time of Franck and Debussy, his music cannot help showing their influences as well as those of Fauré and d'Indy. Baker says of Jongen's music:

> While not pursuing extreme modern effects, Jongen succeeded in imparting an original touch to his harmonic style.[1]

Opus 115 was commissioned for the 1941 concours at the Royal Conservatories at Brussels and Antwerp. The solo is dedicated to Pierre de Leye, Professor of Clarinet at Brussels. This composition and "Reverdies" by René Bernier (1960) are the only two solos chosen for the Paris Conservatory examinations by Belgian composers.

    "Recitativo et Airs de Ballet" is in three large

73

sections: a recitative, without bar lines, gives the
clarinet sweeping arpeggios, with dotted chords of
punctuation in the accompaniment; a dance-like section follows in 6/8, marked "Molto grazioso"; the
last section in 2/4 is marked "Allegro vivo." Writing with lyrical elegance and spontaneity, Jongen
avoids obvious modulation by the use of much chro-
maticism. The florid, neo-romantic style of this
solo presents severe challenges of technical flexibility and exploits the clarinet's full range of
agile and expressive possibilities.

                          1949

Bucolique (6' 40")   EUGENE BOZZA (1905-   )
                              Difficulty: 7*
                              Paris: Leduc

    Eugène Bozza, who was born in Nice, studied
violin, conducting, and composition at the Paris
Conservatory. He won first prizes in 1924 and 1930,
for violin and conducting, respectively. A composition student of Henri Büsser, he was awarded, in
1934, the Grand Prix de Rome. He held a conducting
post at the Opéra Comique in 1939, and later became
the Director of the Conservatoire National at Valenciennes. He composed an opera and several orchestral works in the 1940's. Although attracted strongly to woodwinds, he has also contributed an impres-
sively large number of compositions for string,
brass, and percussion instruments, as well as chamber
music and sacred choral works. A few of Bozza's
earlier woodwind solos have been adapted by the composer for other instruments. Good examples of this
suitability are his "Aria" (1936) and his "Fantaisie
Italienne" (1938), which have also been published
for the bassoon and the saxophone. The English clarinetist, Jack Brymer, says of the latter, "typically
brilliant French style, and a good sense of line."[2]
    Norman Heim assesses the composer's "Suite" (1974)
as follows:

    The writing does not use the full capabilities
    of the instrument as exemplified so beautifully
    in the "Concerto" which is probably his best
    work.[3]

Pierre Wolff summarizes Bozza's style of writing
thus:

> Il gâte un tempérament généreux et d'audacieuses
> trouvailles d'écriture par un excès de facilité.
> (He spoils a generous temperament and audacious
> writing discoveries by an excessive facility.)[4]

"Bucolique" shows off the highly florid capabilities
of the clarinet in an unending brilliance of preludes
and cadenzas. George Knight says of this work:

> The techniques of impressionism are used in
> writing this composition. Whole-tone scales
> and chromatic scales are the bases for melodic
> construction with diatonic scales noticeably
> absent. These same elements occur in the har-
> monic organization with seventh and ninth chords
> being extracted from them. The resulting chords
> provide a strikingly dissonant background (sec-
> onds, imperfect intervals) for the rapid clari-
> net scale lines.[5]

The following compositions by Bozza are published by Leduc, unless otherwise indicated:

14 Etudes de mécanisme, 1948 (7-8*).
12 Etudes, 1953 (8*).
11 Etudes sur des Modes Karnatiques (8*).
Aria, 1936 (5*).
Ballade. Southern, 1939 (bass clarinet and piano).
Caprice-Improvisation (6-7*).
Claribel, 1952 (6*).
Concerto, 1952 (clarinet and orchestra or piano,
    8*).
Contrastes III, 1977 (clarinet and bassoon, 5-6*).
Divertissement, Opus 39. Southern, 1939 (trans-
    cribed from the English horn solo and dedi-
    cated to Albert Andraud, by D. Hite).
Epithalame. Billaudot.
Fantaisie Italienne, 1938 (6*).
Graphismes, 1975 (preparation for the reading of
    contemporary notation, unaccompanied, 8*).
Idylle (3*).
Prélude et Divertissement (6*).
Pulcinella (7*).
Suite, 1974 (6*).

Trois Mouvements, 1976 (flute and clarinet, 6*).
Rhapsodie Nicoise, 1977 (to A. Dufour, 11',
    7-8*).

1950

(also selected for 1959)

Concertino, Opus 15   JEANINE RUEFF (1922-   )
    (7' 20")   Difficulty: 8*
    Clarinet and piano   Paris: Leduc
    or orchestra

A composer and professor at the Conservatoire,
Jeanine Rueff studied with Henri Büsser and won the
Grand Prix de Rome in 1948. She has written six
solos de concours for other wind instruments plus
four works for the saxophone. Londeix quotes two
French writers about her music:

    Musicienne d'élégance, d'esprit, de finesse et
    parfois d'humour. (Musician of elegance, spirit,
    refinement and sometimes wit.)[6]
    Musique généreuse, adroitement construite. (Gen-
    erous music, adroitly constructed.)[7]

An annotated listing by Tuthill, describes Concertino
as "one of the better Conservatoire-type pieces."[8]
    The first section, "Allegro" (3/4), contains bold
chromatic chord changes in the piano and quick patterns of sixteenth notes and triplets in the solo
instrument. An "Adagio" section builds softly from
the chalumeau register to a long cadenza which leads
directly into the third section, "Allegro" (2/4).
This concluding rondo is not without problems at the
speed indicated by the composer, because of frequent
meter changes to 3/8 and many sixteenth-note triplet
figures. Aside from this ensemble problem, the
piano part does not present a great amount of difficulty, compared to some of the other clarinet solos
of this era.
    Other clarinet works:

    15 Etudes. Leduc (7-8*).
    Variazioni. Leduc, 1976 (8*).
    Hommage à J. S. Bach. Billaudot, 1977.
        (from collection directed by Guy Dangain).

Cinq Pièces pour Clarinette et piano. Billaudot,
1978 (in the style de Couperin, Rameau,
Haydn, Clementi and Schumann, from collection directed by Guy Dangain).

1951

Scherzo (7' 45")   GEORGES HUGON (1904-   )
                              Difficulty: 7
                              Paris: Billaudot

After studying at the Conservatoire, Hugon was
the Director of the Conservatoire at Boulogne-sur-
Mer from 1934 to 1941. In 1941, he became a professor at the Conservatoire National in Paris. His
most successful composition was the oratorio, Au
Nord (1930). He also wrote two symphonies (1941
and 1949) and two symphonic poems. Dumesnil points
out that the composer had less success with one of
these works, Le Ballet de la Reine Raba:

On percevait trop nettement l'influence de son
maître Paul Dukas. (It showed too neatly the
influence of his master, Paul Dukas.)[9]

His chamber music, songs, and various pieces for
piano show "writing with elegance."[10]
    In the Scherzo for clarinet, one will find in-
fluences of impressionism as well as bitonal textures. Although this is not an inspiring solo, the
composer writes with good understanding of the clarinet, using melodic interest and a variety of rhythmic activity to make interesting study material.

1952

Fantaisie (7' 30")   PIERRE REVEL (1901-   )
                              Difficulty: 8*
                              Paris: Leduc

At the Conservatoire National de Musique Supérieur, Pierre Revel studied organ and piano with
Marcel Dupré and Louis Vierné. He won first prizes
in Harmony, Fugue, Piano Accompanying, and Composition. His professors in composition were Charles
Widor, Paul Dukas, and Jean Gallon. Later he taught

at the Conservatoire. His compositions include solo
works for piano, organ, and harp, in addition to
chamber music for various combinations. His woodwind works are Five Pieces, Eglogue, and Petite
Suite for flute, oboe and bassoon, respectively.

Fantaisie for clarinet is divided into three
parts--"Prélude," "Andante," and "Final." An ex-
tended cadenza between the second and third parts
is a real showpiece for the clarinet. In a "Performance Analysis of Selected Compositions," Caringi says:

> Prélude. The opening of the solo is quite free,
> almost giving the impression of extemporized
> music. A motif is played by the clarinet at
> measures 4 and 5 which is the basis of the en-
> tire 26-measure section.
> Andante. The composer again employs material
> generating from but one source. In this case
> it is more extended and, in fact, could be des-
> cribed as a theme.
> Final. Containing an Allegro, Meno mosso and
> Tempo I is, of the entire solo, the only sec-
> tion in which a formal design may be perceived.
> . . . Revel's composition places rigorous de-
> mands on the technical dexterity of the clari-
> netist. The well-trained and experienced per-
> former, equipped with a sound finger technique,
> may meet these demands through careful study.[11]

1953

Concerto   HENRI TOMASI (1901-1971)
    I. Allegro giocoso   Difficulty: 8*
       (7' 40")   Paris: Leduc
    Clarinet and piano
    or orchestra
    (see also 1966)

A composer and conductor of Corsican descent,
Tomasi studied with Vidal and d'Indy and won the
Second Prix de Rome in 1927. He served as Music
Director of the Paris Radio, in French Indochina
(1930-35), and also conducted opera in Monte Carlo
(1946-50). To translate Tomasi's own views on his
music:

My musical knowledge is not based on any system.
The sensibility expresses itself and the mind
controls. What good is it to invent new forms
of speech? Everything has been said and everything has been done.[12]

Tomasi wrote three operas, six ballets, ten orchestral pieces, and five concertos. About his operas
Golea says:

He is a traditional, tonal composer with a great
freedom of expression who often borrows very successfully from folklore and who has a sure sense
of dramatic effect that crown his lyric outbursts
with a fine glow, a great clarity of expression.[13]

Although the Concerto for clarinet is not well known
in America, three writers have made some interesting
comments about this work. Tuthill, in his annotated
listing, says, "A spirited up-to-date work requiring
complete technical facility. Musical, reasonably
worthwhile."[14] About the tonality, Knight says:

Tomasi employs traditional key centers, but he
uses them within a flexible framework which per-
mits the introduction of several untraditional
elements. Many sections are polychordal and
several appear as brief harmonic intrusions. .
. . The chords built on thirds extend beyond
traditional seventh chords to the point of extreme dissonance. In the clarinet part, keys
are discernible, but the line is characterized
by rapidly shifting tonal centers and free re-
lationships between keys.[15]

On the technical aspects of the concerto's first
movement, Caringi observes:

The extreme demands imposed by the composer are
not for the purpose of pyrotechnic display. Rather, they are the result of the composer's use
of the contemporary idiom in creating a musical
work of art.[16]

Although the classic concerto conventionally begins
with a tutti exposition, Tomasi's begins with a
clarinet statement from each of the three themes of

the first movement followed by a development sec-
tion and a long cadenza.
   Other solo works for clarinet, published by
Leduc:

   Chant Corse, 1932 (4*).
   Complainte du Jeune Indian, 1949 (4*).
   Danse Nuptiale for clarinet and piano or orches-
      tra (from numbers 4 and 5 of Danses Profanes
      et Sacrées, 6-7*).
   Introduction et Danse, 1949 (clarinet or saxo-
      phone with piano or orchestra, dedicated to
      Louis Cahuzac, 7*).
   Sonatine Attique (clarinet unaccompanied, 7*).
   4 Divertissements 1964 (four clarinets).
   Divertimento Corsica (oboe, clarinet and bassoon
      with strings and harp or piano).

                          1954

Concerto Lyrique (8')   ALAIN BERNAUD (1932-   )
   I. Allegro Giusto   Difficulty: 8*
   Clarinet and piano   Paris: Leduc
   or orchestra

   Bernaud has five first prize Diplomas from the
Conservatoire--Composition (class of Tony Aubin),
Fugue and Counterpoint (classes of Noël Gallon),
Harmony (class of J. de la Presle), and composition
for Organ. In 1957, he won the Premier Grand Prix
de Rome; since then he has written many solos and
concertos for various instruments, as well as orchestral and chamber works. He is Professor of
Harmony, Counterpoint, and Analysis at the Ecole
Normale de Musique and also a Professor of Solfège
at the Conservatoire National Supérieur.
   About his style of musical composition, Bernaud
says:

   I do not sacrifice my expression to a particular
   system of musical language. I also do not deny
   my affiliation to the tonal music any more than
   to the influences of Bartók, Honegger, Proko-
   fieff or Dutilleux.[17]

Burnet Tuthill lists the Concerto Lyrique and says:

A quite up-to-date test piece for the Paris
Conservatoire and of more musical value than
most of such works. Requires very advanced
technique and musicianship.[18]

The other movements of the concerto are marked as
follows:

II. Lento sostenuto (4' 30").
III. Vivo e giocoso (7' 30").

Other clarinet solos:

Romance. Rideau Rouge (easy-medium).
Récitative et Air. Leduc, 1958 (7*).
Phantasmes. Rideau Rouge (see 1970).

1955

Fantaisie et Danse en Forme de Gigue (6' 35")	JULES SEMLER-COLLERY (1902-) Difficulty: 8* Paris: Leduc

Semler-Collery was a student of Paul Vidal and
Vincent d'Indy and later became Chief Director of
Navy Bands. "His works carry the mark of their au-
thor--frankness, expression of harmonic content,
virtuosity in writing always ringing clear."[19]
The 1955 solo by this composer is written in
traditional style with a few interesting chromatic
progressions and florid passages idiomatically written for the clarinet. The light staccato of the
Danse en Forme de Gigue furnishes some needed variety
and also contains a return of the Fantaisie theme.
While the composer shows great understanding in writing for the clarinet, this work seems too obvious,
with nothing new or refreshing to say.
Other clarinet works:

Rêverie et Scherzo. Leduc, 1950 (7*).
Etudes de Concert. Eschig (medium difficulty).
Pièce de Caractère. Billaudot, 1975 (in classic
    style, medium difficulty, 6').
Cantabile et Allegro. Billaudot, 1967 (easy).

1956

Duo Concertant (7' 15")   DARIUS MILHAUD (1892-1974)
                           Difficulty: 7
                           Paris: Heugel

Milhaud, who came from an old Jewish family in
Aix-en-Provence, developed his personal style at an
early age and became the most prolific 20th-century
French composer, with a catalogue of well over 400
compositions. At the Conservatoire, from 1909 to
1915, he studied Violin, Harmony, Counterpoint and
Fugue; his professor of composition was Charles
Widor. Milhaud and his fellow French composers of
the Groupe des Six are usually credited with being
pioneers of polytonality. However, in Modern French
Music, Myers points out:

> It was the example of Charles Koechlin that ins-
> pired them. . . . Long before Milhaud had
> started to compose, Koechlin had written his
> viola sonata (1913-15) which he described as
> "uninhibitedly bitonal."[20]

(This sonata was dedicated to Milhaud, who gave the
first performance).
Milhaud did not resort to dissonance and the
polytonal idiom in a haphazard fashion, but studied
its theory, in relation to both harmony and counterpoint. In an article written in 1923, Hill says,
"Milhaud has obviously derived his inspiration in
this direction [polyharmonic writing] chiefly from
Stravinsky."[21]
Milhaud has left a rich legacy of chamber music
employing the clarinet, in addition to five solo
works. He was sixty-four when he wrote the last solo,
for the 1956 concours. Like other composers of the
older generation who have continued to write according to the aesthetics and techniques of their youth,
he evolved an interesting piece which is firmly
rooted in tonality. At times, the accompaniment appears to be slightly dissonant and polytonal with
effects created through the use of cluster-like
chords. These chords, however, are still built
around a definite tonal center, with the dissonant
tones serving only as mild disguises for the func-
tional chord movement. Knight, in his dissertation

on 20th-century clarinet materials, discusses Duo
Concertant as follows:

> At times the dissonant tones are found to be an-
> ticipation of harmonies encountered in subsequent
> adjacent chords. . . . Melodies are generally
> constructed with smooth lines featuring a grace-
> ful rise and fall. A particularly striking ex-
> ception is found in the 6/8 section. Here, this
> slow and expressive melody is characterized by
> constantly repeated major and minor tenths, which
> are written as octave transpositions.[22]

Other clarinet solos:

Sonatine, Opus 100. Durand, 1927 (for L. Cahuzac).
Scaramouche. Durand, 1939 (transcribed by the
    composer from the saxophone solo).
Concerto, Opus 230. Elkan Vogel, 1941 (commis-
    sioned by Benny Goodman, but never performed
    by him).
Caprice. International, 1953.

                              1957

Concertino (7' 15")   DESIRE DONDEYNE (1921-   )
                                 Difficulty: 7*
                                 Paris: Leduc

Désiré Dondeyne now serves as conductor of the
Musique des Gardiens de la Paix, a concert band in
Paris. At the Conservatoire, he studied with Aubin,
Rivier, and Milhaud, and won First Prize Diplomas
in Chamber Music, Clarinet, Harmony, Counterpoint,
Fugue, and Composition. His compositions include
works for orchestra, chamber music, and solos. The
melodic lyricism of his music expands in a style of
tonal and modal elements with rhythmic patterns
which are uncomplicated.
    George Wahn, who attended the 1957 concours du
Conservatoire, says of the Concertino:

> After hearing it played in Paris by eight of
> Professor Delécluse's finalists and after work-
> ing on the number myself, I conclude that it is
> a good technic piece but musically lacking.[23]

The work consists of an opening allegro, a cadenza,
an andante in 3/8, and an allegro in 2/4.
Other clarinet works:

Romance. Leduc, 1958 (4-5*).
Triptyque. Transatlantiques, 1969 (accompaniment
        for piano or strings and two harps, 9').
9 Grands Duos Concertants. Transatlantiques
        (two clarinets).

1958

Variations (8' 30")   VICTOR SERVENTI (1907-   )
                                 Difficulty: 7-8*
                                 Paris: Leduc

    Victor Serventi was born in Algiers. While
studying at the Conservatoire National Supérieur de
Musique, he obtained first prize Diplomas in Piano
(1928) and Harmony (1933), and First Honorable Mention in Composition (1936).
    An expressive, sustained theme of four-measure
phrases, marked "Grave et libre," is presented in
the piano. At the end of each phrase, the clarinet
plays a short dialogue of an improvised nature. The
basic key of E-flat contains chords with added notes;
these 7ths, 9ths, and 6ths give a rather sweet and
commercial sound to traditional harmonizations. Both
the clarinet and piano parts have well-written passages which demand fluency, and the clarinet is
called upon to play altissimo A-flat, A, and B-flat
quite often.
    The five interesting variations in different
moods are as follows:

    I.   Allegro (♩ = 108)

    II. Souple et balancé (♩ = 66)

    III. Andante espressivo (♩ = 60), blues
              feeling

    IV. Scherzando (♩ = 116)

    V.   Lent (♩ = 50), very florid

A short cadenza leads to a brilliant coda which
is followed by a soft and peaceful ending.

1959

Concertino, Opus 15   JEANINE RUEFF (1922-   )
   (see 1950)

1960

Reverdies (8')   RENE BERNIER (1905-   )
   Clarinet and piano   Difficulty: 8*
      or orchestra   Paris: Leduc

A pupil of Gilson, Bernier taught at the Liège
Conservatory and later became a supervisor of music
schools in Brussels. He was one of the original
members of the Belgian group of composers called
"Synthétistes" whose aim was to combine modern technique with classic forms. While he is representa-
tive of the contemporary Belgian School, his music
shows more French influence than Flemish character.
In addition to numerous pieces of chamber music and
choruses, he wrote two orchestral works (1933 and
1947) and an oratorio. His piece "Hommage à Sax"
(Leduc), was used for the saxophone concours of 1958.
   Bruce Lobaugh says that:

   "Reverdies" is in a style typical of a good many
   pieces of this era--romantic harmony, expressive
   slow passages contrasted with brilliant ones,
   with even more technical demands.[24]

The work has been recorded in Brussels on Buffet-
Crampon Records (DB 94).

1961

Air Tendre et Varié   JEAN HUBEAU (1917-   )
   (7' 36")   Difficulty: 7
                           Paris: Durand

   Hubeau entered the Conservatoire at the age of

nine and won the First Prize for piano at thirteen.
After that, he studied composition with Jean and
Noël Gallon and Paul Dukas.   In 1934, he received
the Second Grand Prix de Rome.   Hubeau traveled in
Europe as a concert pianist until 1942, when he was
appointed Director of the Conservatoire at Versailles.
He has written three ballets, a symphonic poem, concertos for violin, cello, and piano, much chamber
music, choral works, songs, and piano pieces.

The seven-page solo for clarinet begins with an
"Andantino tranquillo" (6/8 and 8/8).   The variation takes the performer through several fast and
slow tempo changes before returning to a tranquil
ending.   The music is bitonal and offers a challenge
for ensemble between piano and clarinet because of
abrupt changes in rhythmic patterns and chromatic
sequences.

Other work including clarinet:

    Sonatine. Billaudot (flute, clarinet, horn, and
        piano).

1962

Pièce de Concours, Opus   RENE CHALLAN (1910-   )
  56 (4' 30")   Difficulty: 6
                         Paris: Choudens

Not to be confused with his older brother,
Henri, who is a distinguished professor at the Conservatoire, René Challan was a pupil of Noël Gallon
and Henri Büsser.   He was awarded the Grand Prix de
Rome in 1935 and has written mostly chamber music
and smaller works.

The "Pièce de Concours," shows a good knowledge
of techniques of the composer's trade.   However,
the three-page clarinet part contains diatonic and
chordal patterns and presents no new or exciting
difficulties.   The background accompaniment exhibits
nothing more than sequential patterns with some
chromatic movement.   At times, the parallel motion
of the chords achieve some contemporary effects.
It should be noted this solo is considerably less
difficult than many of the other diploma solos of
the 1960's.

                              1963

Sonatine (7' 30")   PIERRE SANCAN (1916-   )
                               Difficulty: 8
                               Paris: Durand

    After winning first prizes in piano, harmony,
and composition at the Conservatoire, Sancan was
awarded the Grand Prix de Rome in 1943. He had a
brilliant career as a concert pianist, which took
him throughout the world; in 1956, he became Professor of Piano at the Conservatoire, followed by his
appointment, in 1963, to the Conseil Supérieur of
that institution. Since 1950, he has composed numerous works for piano solo, three concertos for
piano, an opera, and a ballet. He has written several sonatines for flute (1955), oboe (1959), and
violin (1961)--and a very whimsical examination piece
for the saxophone in 1973, entitled "Lamento et
Rondo."
    Written in one movement, the "Sonatine for Clar-
inet and Piano" contains a ternary form in each of
the three sections, which are marked "Allegro," "Andante sostenuto," and "Vivo." The work contains lush
harmonies and a pleasant use of dissonance with some
humorous rhythmic effects. It is an enjoyable piece
for the performers as well as the audience.

                              1964

Trois Légendes   CLAUDE PASCAL (1921-   )
    I. de la Montagne   Difficulty: 7-8
       (4' 10")   Paris: Durand
   II. des Etages de Choey
       (2' 30")
  III. des Pirinpillins
       (1' 30")

    A music critic for Le Figaro, Pascal is Artistic
Director and Professor of Sight-singing at the Conservatoire. He studied with Tony Aubin and Henri
Büsser and won the Grand Prix de Rome in 1945. About
his music, Robert Bernard says:

    It is the qualities of freshness, spontaneity,

good humor, that distinguish the way of C. P.
His writing is brilliant, harmonies seductive,
and it is with a rare ability that he utilizes
the possibilities of the different instruments.25

The first movement of the "Trois Légendes" is,
in the opinion of this writer, too long; it could be
cut or eliminated in a recital. The second and third
movements, however, provide great contrast which
could be a welcome addition to any program of clarinet music. The slow second movement has lush color
and paints a gentle mood, while the third is an exciting "Presto" with some interesting cross rhythms.
Other clarinet solos:

6 Pièces Variées. Durand (med. difficult).
Lanterne Magique. Billaudot, 1977 (med. diffi-
    cult, from the collection directed by Guy
    Dangain).

1965

Dialogues, Opus 92   MARCEL MIHALOVICI
    (8')   (1898-   )
    I. Poco lento e   Difficulty: 9
       improvisando   Paris: Heugel
   II. Allegro assai

A prolific composer, Mihalovici was born in Rumania and came to study with Vincent d'Indy at the
Schola Cantorum. He remained in Paris and was one
of the "Triton Group" of composers. His major works
include three operas, nine orchestral compositions,
chamber music, and a number of pieces for solo instruments. His style and melodic material often sug-
gest that of Hindemith, though usually with greater
dissonance and less logic. About the composer's
style in the reed Trio, Opus 71, James Gillespie
says, "Multimeters, atonality and rhythmic vitality
characterize the style."26
Another American writer, Huot Fischer, says this
about Mihalovici's clarinet solos:

The works of Mihalovici are among the most difficult of the French woodwind-style solos and
display a twentieth-century disregard for tra-

ditional consonance. It is doubtful whether the
musical results justify the efforts to overcome
the technical difficulties presented to the
performer.[27]

"Dialogues" is highly dissonant, and it does
not adhere to any particular twentieth-century system of tonality. The first movement has frequent
meter changes and florid passages in the clarinet
which are imitated occasionally in the piano. The
second movement is a rondo and contains a long and
difficult passage in a quasi-cadenza style.
Other clarinet solos:

Sonata, Opus 35. Salabert, 1933 (E^b, A, and
      bass clarinet trio).
Sonata, Opus 78. Heugel, 1959 (16' 30").
Musique Nocturne. Leduc, 1963 (clarinet and
      piano or orchestra).
Prétextes. Heugel (oboe, bass clarinet, and
      chamber orchestra).
Récit, Opus 101. Billaudot, 1973 (clarinet,
      unaccompanied, dedicated to Guy Dangain).

                      1966

Concerto   HENRI TOMASI (1901-1971)
    II. Nocturne (3')   Difficulty: 7*
   III. Scherzo Final   Paris: Leduc
        (4' 40") clarinet
        and piano or or-
        chestra
    (see 1953)

According to Professor Ulysse Delécluse:

[The "Concerto"] has gained an enormous popularity throughout Europe; many critics regard
it as a contemporary masterpiece for the clarinet.[28]

For this reason, it is quite understandable that
the second and third movements were chosen for the
1966 concours.
The opening theme in the second movement is
characterized by leaps of sevenths and octaves.

The succession of tones is often predictable, according to the key outlines, but the pattern is
frequently interrupted by shifts to unrelated centers of chromatic alterations. Pulsations are regular in their occurrences in both the second and
the third movements. In these movements, combinations of meters (4/4-12/8, 3/4-9/8, and 2/4-6/8)
are used frequently.
Other clarinet works:

(see 1953).

1967

Divertimento Dell'   TONY AUBIN (1907-   )
  Incertezza   Difficulty: 7*
  (7' 15")   Paris: Leduc
  Clarinet and piano
  or strings

Professor of Composition at the Conservatoire
and member of l'Institut de France, Aubin was a
pupil of Paul Dukas and won the Grand Prix de Rome
in 1930. Claude Rostand says:

In his work we discover the influence, well assimilated, of Franck, Dukas, and Ravel. From
Dukas he inherited the love for well-balanced
large forms, Fauré and Ravel, subtle harmonies
and supreme elegance.[29]

Although this solo of 1967 is well-written and
contains a variety of melodic and articulated
styles, it is not an exciting piece for public performance with piano.
Other clarinet solo:

Le Calme de la Mer. Leduc (from the Suite Eo-
  lienne, third movement, Lento 3/4, legato
  style, 4*).

1968

Concerto   IDA GOTKOVSKY (1933-   )
  Finale (10' 30")   Difficulty: 8-9

(with cuts, 7' 30")   Paris: Editions Musicales
                           Transatlantiques

Ida Gotkovsky studied at the Conservatoire National Supérieur, where she was awarded five first
prizes for writing and composition. She is a dis-
ciple of Tony Aubin, Olivier Messiaen, and Nadia
Boulanger. All of her works have been performed,
often as soon as written, by some of the leading
orchestras and soloists of Europe. One of France's
major composers, she has written over thirty-five
large works and has won many honors and prizes for
her compositions, along with many glowing critical
reviews. About her style of writing, two French
writers say:

> Her esthetics reveal a rigorous structure along
> with thematic writing based on impressionism.
> Both of these traits are elaborated with extreme
> virtuosity.[30]
> Clear, direct music, with the ideas flowing
> naturally . . . composition is very refined and
> the instrumentation rich and colorful.[31]

For several successive years, Ida Gotkovsky has
been selected to write competitive works for the
Conservatoire. Her ten concertos with orchestra
include two for clarinet, two for trumpet, one for
saxophone, one for bassoon, and others for stringed
instruments.
The "Finale" of the 1968 Concerto for clarinet
opens with a large pyramid chord, and the first page
is devoted to a brilliant and effective cadenza.
The composer has the ability to build much excitement in the allegro sections by long crescendo and
cross accents. These sections have also contrasting
legato passages, expressively written in the low register. The work is difficult for both clarinet and
piano, but it is well worth the effort.
Other clarinet works:

Dolcissimo. Billaudot, 1977 (contained in a col-
    lection, directed by Guy Dangain, this piece
    is fashioned from Brillance, the third move-
    ment of a 1974 saxophone composition).
Eoloinne. Billaudot, 1979 (clarinet and harp).
Concerto. Billaudot, 1979 (clarinet and strings).

1969

Triptyque (7')   DESIRE DONDEYNE (1921-   )
    Clarinet and piano   Difficulty: 8
    or strings and two   Paris: Transatlantiques
    harps

    (See 1957 for details about the composer and
his other clarinet compositions).
    The "Triptyque" is divided into three Tableaux
which are marked "enchainez" (to be played without
interruption). Tableau I begins quietly (Andante
12/8) with arpeggios in the piano, often employing
augmented octave intervals. The clarinet plays
lines of descending arpeggios in fourths, and after
a brief middle section (Allegro 3/4), the remainder
of the movement is a lyrical Andante which incor-
porates material from previous themes. Tableau II
begins with a quasi cadenza e ad libitum and the
last part is marked "Vivace e capriccioso." Tableau III (Allegro vivace), also in 4/8, is the movement that brings out the clarinetist's technical
ability; it features running triplets leading to
a brilliant ending.
    This composition shows fine idiomatic writing
and contains good technical study material for the
clarinet.

1970

Phantasmes (7' 45")   ALAIN BERNAUD (1932-   )
                            Difficulty: 8
                            Paris: Rideau Rouge

    (See 1954 for details about the composer and
his other clarinet compositions).
    "Phantasmes" is in two movements--Recitativo and
Perpetuum Mobile. The first movement is an ABA form
beginning with chords in fourths and major sevenths
in the accompaniment and long arpeggios in the solo
instrument. The middle section is a lyrical line
for the clarinet and a syncopated accompaniment for
the piano. The second movement, marked "più presto
possibile," contains sixteenth-note patterns in the
clarinet, accompanied by dissonant chords. The contrasting middle section has a melodic line in quar-

ter notes, and the piano furnished harp-like accompaniment.

This work is probably not as rewarding for the clarinetist as the composer's earlier "Concerto Lyrique," of 1954.

Other required solo for 1970:

C. M. von Weber: Grand Duo Concertant (II. Andante and III. Rondo).

1971

Capriccio (4' 45")   CLAUDE ARRIEU (1903-   )
                            Difficulty: 8
                            Paris: Amphion
                            U.S. Agent: Belwin-Mills

Claude Arrieu was a piano student of Marguerite Long; her teachers for writing and composition were Caussade, Gallon, and Ducasse. As a pupil of Paul Dukas, she won the First Prize in Composition at the Conservatoire in 1932. The flexibility of her talent, the natural elegance of her style, and the neatness of her writing won many awards for her compositions. Among her many works are a music drama, three comic operas, and numerous scores of incidental music for radio. Her instrumental music includes two violin concertos, a piano concerto, a flute concerto, a trombone solo, and chamber music.

Arrieu's writing tends to be neoclassic in style, and her textures often feature a tonal idiom with chromatic harmony and abrupt modulations. In review of the 1971 clarinet solo, I wrote:

There are basically two thematic ideas which are introduced early in the slow section and the scherzando. The slow beginning theme of minor thirds, moving chromatically, is about the only expressive material in the solo. This is brought back later in an imitative dialogue in both the piano and the clarinet. The second idea is a scherzando in a 6/8 and 5/8 design. The motive for this is later developed into a short two-part fugue.[32]

Other required solo for 1971:

C. M. von Weber: Concerto No. 2, Opus 74
    (Allegro, 1st movement).

Other clarinet works:

La Fête. Billaudot (easy).
Un jour d'été. Billaudot (easy).
Petit choral. Billaudot (very easy).
5 Mouvements. Billaudot, 1970 (clarinet quartet--
    Eb, 2 Bb, and bass clarinets, 10').
Trio. Amphion (oboe, clarinet, and bassoon).

                        1972

Quatre Paysages Italiens CHRISTIAN MANEN (1934-   )
    1. Du haut du campanile Difficulty: 8
    2. La chapelle aux ifs Paris: Choudens
    3. L'estate
    4. Rome parmi toits
        et coupoles

    Manen studied at the Conservatoire from 1949 to
1961, during which time he won eight first prizes
for Solfège, Harmony, Counterpoint, Fugue, Percussion, Composition, Conducting, and Organ-Improvisa-
tion. In 1961, he won the First Grand Prix de Rome;
he studied and composed in Rome from 1962 to 1965.
Since 1964, he has been Director and Conductor at
l'Ecole de Musique d'Asnières; he has also been a
professor at the Conservatoire National Supérieur
de Paris.
    Translated information about the composer's
style indicates that he is not within the margin of
any particular system or limited by any one means
which would force a monotonous musical expression.
He likes color, feels that all forms of tonality
exist, and thinks there is still much to be said
with traditional materials. He is not living in the
past, nor only in the future; he is a musician of
today.[33]
    Manen has written a number of educational
materials for the Conservatoire, orchestral works,
much chamber music, and about twelve concours
pieces for various instruments.

1973

Diptyque (6')   MICHEL MERLET (1939-   )
    I. Arioso   Difficulty: 8*
    II. Eglogue   Paris: Leduc

Merlet received several diplomas from the Conservatoire. The classes in which he won First
Prizes were Instrumental Ensemble (Oubradous), Fugue
(Desportes), Composition (Aubin), and Musical Ana-
lyses (Messiaen). In 1966, he received the Second
Grand Prix de Rome; he has since been active as a
teacher in several conservatories in the Paris
area.
In 1968, Merlet was commissioned to write educational materials and sight-reading examination
pieces; two years later, he wrote the concours
piece for flute, entitled "Chacone." The composer
has also been commissioned to write for orchestra
and chamber music performances in Caen, Fontaine-
bleau, Melun, Nantes, Nancy, and Rouen.
The following review of "Diptyque" for clarinet
appeared in 1976:

The style of the Arioso for the clarinetist is
florid, almost like a cadenza, while the difficulty of the Eglogue is the speed of the fast
notes. The piano accompaniment is quite difficult and at times scored as if it is a piano
reduction of an instrumental score. The clarinet and piano parts are both difficult, but time
spent on perfecting the parts and the ensemble
will be well rewarded, because the style is at-
tractive and challenging.[34]

Other clarinet work:

Stabile. Leduc (3*).

1974

Tema con Variazioni   JEAN FRANÇAIX (1912-   )
    (6' 45")   Difficulty: 8-9
                                Paris: Eschig

Jean Françaix studied piano with Isidor Philipp
and was a composition pupil and protégé of Nadia
Boulanger. Like Debussy and Milhaud, he has achieved
international fame. Baker says of his music:

> In his music, Fr. associates himself with the
> neo-French school of composers, pursuing the
> twofold air of practical application and na-
> tional tradition; his instrumental works repre-
> sent a stylisation of classical French music;
> in this respect, he comes close to Ravel.[35]

Claude Rostand compares the writing of Jean Françaix to that of Jacques Ibert:

> While his inventiveness does not undergo much
> change, his workmanship testifies to a sur-
> prising facility, so that he can handle much
> with ease and gracefulness. It has been said
> that he is like a son of Jacques Ibert.[36]

After using the clarinet in numerous chamber
music works, Françaix wrote his clarinet concerto
in 1968. This 27-minute work was dedicated to
Ferdinand Oubradous and was first performed by
Jacques Lancelot. It is more successfully played
with orchestra than with the three-line reduction.
Jack Brymer expresses the opinion of many clarinetists:

> Its roulades in the key of B Major are beyond
> almost any player; but the work is a worth-
> while challenge, and the A clarinet would pro-
> bably provide the answer.[37]

"Tema con Variazioni" for clarinet in A is
written in a neoclassical style with many diatonic
and chordal patterns. The theme (Moderato, 7/8)
is identified by the name of the composer's grand-
son, "Olivier," to whom the composition is dedicated.
Showing the elegant style of his writing, Françaix
makes all of the six variations interesting and
varied. The successful performance of his long and
graceful lines requires a smooth execution and control of the technical and rhythmic patterns.
Other required solo for 1974:

Robert Schumann: Fantaisiestücke, Opus 73.

Other clarinet work:

Concerto. Transatlantiques, 1968.

1975

Bagatelle (6')   MARCEL BITSCH (1921-   )
                           Difficulty: 7*
                           Paris: Leduc

Marcel Bitsch studied at the Conservatoire with
Noël Gallon and Henri Büsser and won the Grand Prix
de Rome in 1945. He has written seven orchestral
works, a concerto for piano, and numerous solo works
for winds. The composer's "Pièce Romantique," written in 1950, is described by Knight as follows:

> The work does not appear to be traditionally
> conceived. Some passages are easily defined as
> bitonal (measures 73-75), but most exhibit noth-
> ing more than sequential patterns consisting of
> chromatic movement to a high or lower pitch
> level.[38]

A review of Bitsch's challenging examination piece
of 1975 says:

> It is civilized and charming from its cadenza-
> like opening to the brilliant final presto, set-
> ting, along the way, many a problem in agility
> and rhythm.[39]

Other works for clarinet:

Pièce Romantique. Leduc, 1950 (5*).
12 Etudes de Rythme. Leduc, 1957 (articulations
     and metronome markings by U. Delécluse, 8*).

1976

Variazioni (5' 45")   JEANINE RUEFF (1922-   )
   (see 1950)   Difficulty: 7-8*
                           Paris: Leduc

Six variations and performance styles are derived
from the opening bitonal chords of the first varia-

tion. The fourth and fifth intervals used in the
opening are an important unifying element for the
clarinet and piano parts. The variations are as
follows:

I.   Recitando, 5/4 ($\downarrow$ = 80)
     Piano chords, as stated above, answered by
     arpeggios in the clarinet.

II. Flessibile, 5/16 ($\downarrow\hspace{-0.3em}\downarrow$ = 50)
     Piano plays a rhythmic background in major
     seconds and the clarinet plays running
     scale figures.

III. Rapidamente, 4/4 ($\downarrow$ = 120)
     Fast staccato patterns in short dialogues
     between clarinet and piano.

IV. Espressivo, 3/4 ($\downarrow$ = 60)
     This features a nice expressive counterpoint
     with clarinet and piano.

V.   Volubilmente, 4+5/8 ($\downarrow$ = 176)
     Difficult and chromatic triplet figures for
     the clarinet against an ostinato in the
     piano.

VI. Maestoso ($\downarrow$ = 60)
     A dialogue between clarinet and piano of
     fast arpeggios, makes a loud and rather
     pointless ending.

Variations III and V are marked at exaggerated
tempos and call for flashes of virtuoso performance.
Clarinetists accustomed to Mme. Rueff's earlier
"Concertino" will find the "Variazioni" disjointed
and a bit more austere.
Other required solo for 1976:

C. M. von Weber: Concerto No. 2, Opus 74
     (II. Romance and III. Polacca).

1977

Coïncidence (6' 15")   PIERRE MAX DUBOIS (1930-   )
                              Difficulty: 8*
                              Paris: Leduc

Dubois studied composition at the Conservatoire with Darius Milhaud and Jean Rivier, and in 1955 won the Grand Prix de Rome. He is a Professor of Musical Analysis at the Conservatoire.

Avoiding scholarly formulas and academic means only when it suits him, Dubois guards his liberty in his style of composition and is not a slave to any particular system. Written in a neoclassic style with bits of humor and satire, his music, like that of Jean Français, is clearly defined in a vivacious French spirit. As Jean Cocteau said, "He knows just how far to go, [but not] too far."[40] Having written over 14 compositions for the clarinet, 30 works for the saxophone, and wind ensemble music, Dubois is one of the most prolific composers of music for woodwinds. His easier pieces are interesting and musical for teaching purposes, and his advanced compositions, clever and challenging, are never without audience appeal.

In his 1977 solo de concours, we see a complete change from his earlier style of composition, and it is certainly his most atonal work yet written for the clarinet. The one-movement solo has five varied sections. The first thirteen measures are for clarinet alone; they are marked "Molto vivo (D'un caractère tourmenté et lyrique)." A small chromatic pattern of two notes grows and expands its intervals to an altissimo 'A' at measure 14. The second section continues with the clarinet playing passages of fourths and gradually develops into lyrical phrases with two-part counterpoint with the piano at (6). On the fourth page of the clarinet part, a third section begins in an "Andante" with large skips and a flutter-tongue passage. Also at the end of this section, one sees the first use in an examination solo of multiphonics. These two effects, according to Guy Deplus, "are simple and flat [when played]."[41] The composer indicates that these notes may be optionally cut. Section four returns to the opening "Molto vivo," but not quite as fast as the first section, since there are now more technical patterns of sixteenth notes and triplets. The fifth page is a closing section which resembles section two. In the last eight measures, the clarinet descends softly, unaccompanied.

Other required solo for 1977:

C. M. von Weber: Concerto No. 1 (II. Adagio).

Other clarinet works, published by Leduc, unless otherwise indicated:

12 Studies (medium-difficult).
Romance, 1954 (easy-medium).
Sonatina, 1958 (difficult).
9 Impromptus (medium).
Rhapsodie, 1958 (medium-difficult).
Circus Parade, 1965 (medium-difficult, clarinet
    and percussion).
6 Caprices, 1967 (medium-difficult, two clari-
    nets).
Beaugency Concerto, 1969 ("That rare creation,
    uncomplicated modern French concerto. With
    strings and neoclassical in effect.")42
Menuet (from Beaugency Concerto, easy-medium).
Epitaphe. Rideau Rouge, 1971 (easy).
18 Duos Progressifs. Billaudot, 1975 (easy).
10 Etudes Transcendantes. Billaudot, 1975
    (easy).
Romance sans Paroles. Billaudot, 1977 (easy-
    medium), from the collection directed by
    Guy Dangain.
Quatuor, 1964 (four clarinets).
Virginie. Rideau Rouge, 1969 (easy).
Mini-môme. Billaudot, 1979 (three very easy
    pieces, dedicated to Guy Dangain).

1978

Variations et Hommage   ALAIN MARGONI (1939-   )
    (5' 50")   Difficulty: 8
                             Paris: Editions Françaises
                                 de Musique-Cerda

Margoni studied at the Conservatoire with Tony Aubin, Louis Fourestier, Henri Challan, Maurice Martenot, and Olivier Messiaen. He is now a Professor of Musical Analysis at the Conservatoire National Supérieur de Paris and Director of Music at the Comédie Française. He has composed numerous works for orchestra, solo instruments, and chamber groups.

Sandra Powell, an American who attended the 1978 concours, has this to say about Margoni's clarinet solo:

Variation 1 is a haunting melody with a high
pianissimo tessitura which requires a great
control. Variation 2 is a technical cadenza
beginning at a piano dynamic and building to an
exciting, flashy fortissimo. Variation 3 is a
rhythmic 4/4, 3/4, 5/8 with humorous teamwork
for clarinet and piano. The last variation is
a mysterious one with broken chord color ex-
changes between the instruments. This variation
ends with a rubato clarinet cadenza which leads
into the final Hommage, a beautiful flowing melody in traditional tonality (E-flat). It is the
only tribute in the composition to such tonal-
ity.43

Other required solo for 1978:

Claude Debussy: Première Rhapsodie (see 1910).

Guy Deplus

On June 28, 1978, Guy Deplus was named Professor
of Clarinet at the Conservatoire National Supérieur
de Musique after serving as a professor of sight
reading and later as a professor of woodwind chamber music. Most important for students and clarinetists throughout the world, Monsieur Deplus represents a new direction away from the limited and out-
moded style of playing advocated by the previous
two clarinet professors. As his discography shows,
he is a foremost performing artist whose approach
is musical: he does not stress technique and agility
at the expense of a full, round tone.
Guy Deplus' interest in contemporary music also
marks a radical divergence from the traditionalist
outlook usually favored by most professors at the
Conservatoire. In addition to playing all the
standard classical and romantic clarinet repertoire,
he has spent considerable time performing the newest
French and international compositions. At an early
stage in his career, he was drawn toward new styles
of clarinet literature and became soloist with the
Ensemble Ars Nova and the Domaine Musical. His interest in Pierre Boulez' current work at the Centre
Beaubourg probably will bring about a closer rela-
tionship between the "anti-conservatory" musical

stream and the traditionalist course at the C.N.D.M.
de Paris.

Born in northern France near Valenciennes,
Deplus, after studying two years at the regional
conservatory with Henri Dubois, was admitted to the
Paris Conservatory in 1943. After winning his first
prize for clarinet in 1945 and the first prize in
ensemble in 1946, he studied harmony privately with
Mme Yvonne Desportes and clarinet with Pierre Lefebvre. From 1947 to 1964, he was solo clarinetist
with the Garde Républicaine Band and also performed
with the Concerts Colonne Orchestra. In 1968, he
began to play with the Opéra Comique Orchestra and,
shortly after, became co-principal clarinetist with
the National Opera. As a member of the Octuor de
Paris, and numerous solo appearances, he has gained
worldwide respect as a discerning musician and virtuoso. He has also been invited to perform and teach
at many important European festivals and at the National Clarinet Clinic in Denver, Colorado.

1979

Pastorale et Scherzo   JEAN AUBAIN (1928-   )
   (7' 20")   Difficulty: 8
                            Paris: Amphion

A native of Bordeaux, Aubain first studied at
that city's national conservatory. Among his teachers was Roger Ducasse, who helped him prepare for
both the Conservatoire National Supérieur in Paris
and for the Prix de Rome Concours. In addition to
winning the 1955 Grand Prix de Rome, he also won
first prizes at the Conservatoire in Composition
(class of Tony Aubin), Analysis (class of Olivier
Messiaen), and Counterpoint (class of Simone Pré-
Caussade). Aubain is the Director of the National
Conservatory at Versailles.

The composer describes his music as "melodic and
classic in form with the essence of an enlarged tonality."44 He has composed various sonatas and so-
natinas, published by Leduc and Heugel; his unpublished works include three symphonies and nine works
for student orchestra.

Pastorale et Scherzo, dedicated to Guy Deplus,
Professor at the Conservatoire National Supérieur,
is an easily read, hand-copied reproduction. The

first movement begins and ends with the clarinet in
unaccompanied sections marked "Moderato, senza rigor"
(eighth note = 100). These sections are to be played
avec souplesse (with ease); the measure lines are not
used consistently, and the performer is given some
opportunity for rhythmic and expressive contrasts.
The composer also uses the new notation (slanting
bars) to indicate groups of notes whose speed is to
be increased or decreased. The middle section, a
binary form (ABABA), marked "Allegro inquieto," in
2/4 (quarter note = 152), offers contrasting sections of marcato and warm, smooth styles. Both of
these themes are accompanied by a modified ostinato
beginning with three-measure patterns and changing
later to groups of two measures.

The Scherzo, marked "Allegro marcato" (eighth
note = 200), contains more complexity of rhythm and
great technical difficulty with a number of meter
changes. The movement begins with a dissonant contrapuntal texture in 3/8. The second section contains a number of meter changes with consequently
less contrapuntal variation. The third idea, marked
"molto cantabile, brioso," continues the dissonant
texture in chromatic fifths and fourths. The fourth
section, of eleven measures in 6/4, is considerably
slower and is marked "Molto moderato" (quarter note
= 54). Also marked "Legato e misterioso," it employs
again an ostinato figure in one-measure patterns
which lead abruptly into a return of the first and
second themes. A short coda, fashioned from the
first section, ends the solo softly in the tonality
of D Minor.

                          1980

Sept Figures Magiques   JEAN-PAUL HOLSTEIN
   (9' 30")   (1939-   )
                             Difficulty: 8
                             Paris: Eschig

From the great composers with whom he studied
(Georges Hugon, Jean Rivier, André Jolivet, and
Olivier Messiaen), Jean-Paul Holstein inherited a
style for melodic clarity, rhythmic freedom, and
richness of harmonic textures. From 1962 to 1978,
he won six first prizes at the Conservatoire--Har-
mony (Hugon), Contrepoint and Fugue (Bitsch), Ana-

lysis (Messiaen), Esthetics (Beaufils), and Composition (Rivier and Jolivet). In addition to a doctor-
ate at the Sorbonne and other honors in France, he
received the William and Norma Copley Foundation
Award (Chicago, 1965).

Holstein has taught at the University of Paris
IV-Sorbonne since 1969 and served as Professor of
Analysis (1973 to 1978) and Counterpoint (since 1878)
at the C.N.S.M. of Paris. He has written over one
hundred compositions for all mediums and many of his
works have been published by Billaudot, Choudens,
Heugel, and Leduc. According to his own statement,
"[the composer] feels the great necessity to dedicate
himself to lyricism without renouncing the newest
creative innovations."[45]

In the 1980 solo de concours, each of the seven
figures ends softly, numbers IV and VI are for unaccompanied clarinet, and the composition calls for
the full range of the solo instrument. There are
many tonal effects for both clarinet and piano which
are discussed in the following analysis:

I. Reflets de Nuit, (♩ = 60, Reflections of
    Night)
    The piano begins with dissonant chords, while
    the clarinet plays sustaining notes in the
    middle and low range. Eight-measure sections
    build to measure nineteen, calling for the
    altissimo notes of G-sharp, A, B-flat, B, and
    C; however, these difficult sustained notes
    are only suggested as options. This middle
    section, quite syncopated and loud, leads to
    the clarinet's free 12-tone melody and a pro-
    gressively soft ending.

II. Aurore, comme un froissement, (♩ = 80, Dawn,
    like a rustling)
    The clarinet plays sixteenth-note triplets
    alone for twelve measures, ending with breath
    sounds on the middle A. An eight-measure
    middle section, twice as slow, exploits soft,
    sustained sounds in the clarinet's high range
    against the lowest notes of the piano. In the
    last four measures, the clarinet returns to
    fast rustling notes resembling the beginning
    of the movement.

III. Les Feux du Matin, (♩ = 120, The Morning
     Lights)
     A rather active movement for both instruments
     leads to tremolo passages for the clarinet in
     the last half of the movement with pointal-
     listic accents in the piano.

IV. Midi, quelque chose de brûlant (Midday,
    something that is burning)
    A cadenza movement for clarinet with a three-
    part design. The middle section is strict
    and rhythmic with bar lines and five diffi-
    cult multiple sonorities for the clarinet.
    A short return of the first melodic idea of-
    fers a slight variation.

V. Les Braises du Soir, son plat (♩ = 42, The
   Embers of Evening, with even-dull sound)
   A feeling of tranquility is created by sustained tones in the clarinet against tremolos
   and grace-note arpeggios in the piano. A middle section introduces two more multiple son-
   orities leading to a loud, three-measure ostinato in quarter notes for the piano. This
   movement, with interesting tonal effects,
   fades quietly as both instruments sustain
   trills.

VI. Crépuscule (♩ = 72, Twilight)
    A two-part form for unaccompanied clarinet
    calls for irregular melodic accents to be
    played against fast chromatic figures in the
    first half, followed by evenly accented eighth
    notes over quickly articulated low notes.

VII. Le Jour en Miettes (♩ = 132, The Day in
     Particles)
     A seven-measure ostinato is used four times
     in the piano, and in the third and fourth rep-
     etition the clarinet is featured in short
     chromatic fragments of irregular accents and
     large skips. The second half of the movement
     changes the range to the treble clef with the
     ostinato theme inverted and again used four
     times. During this latter half, the clarinet
     plays glissando passages with suggested rhyth-

mic impulses. A four-measure coda for clarinet ends the composition.

Other required solo for 1980:

Robert Schumann: Fantaisiestücke, Opus 73.

Other clarinet compositions:

Les Duettistes clari-et-nette. Leduc (two clar-
    inets, 3' 10").
Douce-Amère (flute, oboe, clarinet, 3' 15").
Blues et Charleston (clarinet quartet, 6').
Chansons de Flûte. Leduc (clarinet and piano,
    14' 40").
12 Etudes, d'après des modes arabes. Billaudot
    (clarinet solo, 35' 10").
Fulgurance (clarinet and piano, commissioned by
    C.N.S.M. de Paris, 3').
Lancinance (clarinet solo, commissioned by
    C.N.S.M. de Paris, 3').

Conclusion

With the 1980 diploma solo, this annotated study
of the commissioned clarinet solos for the Conservatoire National Supérieur de Musique de Paris comes
to a close. Since 1897, the literature for clarinet
and piano has undergone a development of forms and
styles by skilled musicians, working in close contact with fine clarinetists. The composers commissioned to write the solo de concours--first influenced by nineteenth-century romantic opera and then
by twentieth-century trends of impressionism, bito-
nalism, neo-classicism, and atonalism--have produced
an interesting and varied evolution of creativeness
in an important body of clarinet solo literature.

Notes

INTRODUCTION

1. George Wahn, "Conservatoire National de Paris," The Instrumentalist, XII (September, 1957), 99.
2. This opinion was stated by Guy Deplus in a conversation with the writer in Paris, May, 1974.
3. Edward B. Hill, Modern French Music (New York: Da Capo Press, 1924), 30.

CHAPTER 1: A BRIEF HISTORICAL BACKGROUND

1. Joseph Caringi, "The Clarinet Contest Solos of the Paris Conservatory" (unpublished Ed. D. dissertation, Columbia University, 1963), 4.
2. Oskar Kroll, The Clarinet (New York: Taplinger Publishing Co., 1968), 63.
3. Pamela Weston, More Clarinet Virtuosi of the Past (London: Halstan & Co., 1977), 108.
4. Kroll, op. cit., 68.
5. Geoffrey Rendall, The Clarinet (New York: Philosophical Library, Inc., 1954), 86.
6. Kroll, op. cit., 100.
7. Rendall, op. cit., 98.
8. Kroll, op. cit., 100.
9. Guy Dangain, A propos de la Clarinette, (Paris: Gérard Billaudot, 1978), 48.
10. From a letter addressed to the writer, by Lester Warren, Alphonse Leduc, Paris, March 20, 1979.

11. David Whitwell, A New History of Wind
Music (Evanston: The Instrumentalist Co., 1972),
45.
12. Daniel Bonade, "Henri Lefebvre," The Clarinet, I, 4 (Winter, 1950-51), 26.
13. Keith Stein, quoted in Larry Maxey, "The
Rose Thirty-two Etudes," The Clarinet, I, 4 (August, 1974), 9.

CHAPTER 2: INFLUENCE OF OPERA

1. Henri Rabaud, quoted in Hill, Modern French
Music (New York: Da Capo Press, 1924), 13.
2. Hill, op. cit., 12.
3. Whitwell, op. cit., 45.
4. Bonade, op. cit., 26.
5. Ibid., 26-27.
6. Ibid., 27.
7. Pamela Weston, More Clarinet Virtuosi of
the past (London: Halstan & Co., 1977), 63.

CHAPTER 3: ANNOTATED BIBLIOGRAPHY OF CLARINET
            SOLOS FROM 1897 TO 1918

1. Romain Rolland, Musicians of Today (New
York: Henry Holt and Co., 1915), 259.
2. Joseph Caringi, "The Clarinet Contest Solos
of the Paris Conservatory" (unpublished Ed. D. dissertation, Columbia University, 1963), 110.
3. Ibid., 125.
4. Ibid., 154.
5. Martin Cooper, French Music (London: Oxford
University Press, 1951), 123.
6. Baker's Biographical Dictionary of Musicians
(New York, 1965), 728.
7. James Collis, "Rabaud's 'Solo de Concours,'"
The Clarinet, I, 8 (Winter, 1951-52), 13.
8. Caringi, op. cit., 75.
9. Cooper, op. cit., 202.
10. Earl Boyd, "New Releases--Music," NACWPI
Bulletin, IV, 1 (October, 1955), 4.
11. Caringi, op. cit., 131.
12. Oskar Kroll, The Clarinet (New York: 1968,
Taplinger Publ. Co.), 84.

13. The 1941 edition by Leduc has a cadenza added by the composer.

14. Edward B. Hill, Modern French Music (New York: Da Capo Press, 1924), 187.

15. Letter addressed to the writer, by the Bibliothèque Nationale du Conservatoire de Musique, July 11, 1977.

16. Letter addressed to the writer, by Claude Gitteau, SACEM, Sept. 1, 1977.

CHAPTER 4:   THE PERIOD BETWEEN THE WORLD WARS

1. Rollo Myers, Modern French Music (New York: Praeger Publisher, 1971), 199.

2. Jack Brymer, Clarinet (New York: The Macmillan Co., 1977), 218.

3. Elise Kuhl Kirk, "Three Neglected Composers," The Musical Quarterly, LXIV, 2 (April, 1978), 299.

4. From a letter addressed to the writer by Mme Li-Koechlin, L'Hay-les-Roses, France, June 22, 1976.

5. Russell Landgrabe, "Letters to the Editor," The Clarinet, V.3 (Spring, 1978), 6.

6. Henri Barraud, Dictionary of Contemporary Composers, John Vinton, ed. (New York: E. P. Dutton, 1974), 250-251.

7. George Townsend, "Clarinet Reviews," Woodwind World, XVII, 5 (Nov.-Dec., 1978), 27.

8. Pierre Bernac, Francis Poulenc (New York: W. W. Norton & Co., 1977), 29.

9. Pamela Weston, More Clarinet Virtuosi of the Past (London: Halstan & Co., 1977), 63.

10. Ibid., 64.

11. Pierre Wolff, Musique Contemporaine (Paris: Fernand Nathan, 1954), 198.

12. Rosario Mazzeo, "A Guide to Scale Studies," Selmer Bandwagon (Booklet, reprinted, 1969), 4.

13. Kroll, op. cit., 104.

CHAPTER 5:   ANNOTATED BIBLIOGRAPHY OF CLARINET
             SOLOS FROM 1919 to 1947

1. George W. Knight, "A Comparative Study of Compositional Techniques Employed in Instructional Materials and Twentieth Century Solos for Clarinet"

(unpublished dissertation, University of Illinois, 1973), 97-98.

2. M. Pereyra, quoted in 125 Ans de Musique pour Saxophone, ed. J. M. Londeix (Paris: Leduc, 1971), 116.

3. Burnet C. Tuthill, "The Concertos for Clarinet," Journal of Research in Music Education, Vol. 10, No. 1 (Spring, 1962), 51.

4. Baker's Biographical Dictionary of Musicians (New York, 1963), 1248.

5. Groves Dictionary of Music and Musicians (London: Macmillan & Co., 1954), 703.

6. E. Vuillermoz, quoted in Londeix, op. cit., 41.

7. Claude Rostand, French Music Today (New York: Da Capo Press, 1973), 94.

8. Baker, op. cit., 1034.

9. F. Goldberg, "Henri Martelli," Grove's Dictionary, op. cit., 590.

10. N. Dufourcq, quoted in Londeix, op. cit., 105.

11. R. Bernard, Ibid., 105.

CHAPTER 6: AFTER WORLD WAR II

1. Baker, op. cit., 406.

2. Claude Rostand, French Music Today (New York: Da Capo Press, 1973), 40.

3. Myers, op. cit., 157.

4. Olivier Messiaen, Quatuor pour la fin du Temps, from the record jacket (STU 70156, ERATO, Gravure Universelle).

5. A. Golea, "French Music Since 1945," Contemporary Music in Europe (New York: G. Schirmer, 1965), 24.

6. Ibid., 36.

7. Caringi, op. cit., 88.

8. David Weber, "Clarinetists of Paris, "The Clarinet, XVI (Fall, 1954), 5.

CHAPTER 7: ANNOTATED BIBLIOGRAPHY OF CLARINET
            SOLOS FROM 1948 to 1980

1. Baker, op. cit., 791.

2. J. Brymer, Clarinet (New York: Macmillan, 1977), 213.

3. Norman Heim, "Reviews of Clarinet Music," NACWPI Journal (XXIII, 4, Summer, 1975), 37.

4. Pierre Wolff, quoted in Londeix, op. cit., 46.

5. George Knight, op. cit., 65.

6. C. Rostand, quoted in Londeix, op. cit., 217.

7. B. Gavoty, Ibid., 217.

8. B. Tuthill, "The Concertos for clarinet," The Journal of Research in Music Education (X,1, Spring, 1962), 55.

9. René Dumesnil, La Musique en France entre les deux Guerres (Paris: Milieu du Monde), 209.

10. Ibid.

11. Caringi, op. cit., 90, 91, 101.

12. H. Tomasi, quoted in Londeix, op. cit., 240.

13. A. Golea, "French Music since 1945," Contemporary Music in Europe: A Comprehensive Survey, P. H. Lang and N. Broder, eds. (New York: G. Schirmer, 1965) 35.

14. B. Tuthill, op. cit., 57.

15. G. Knight, op. cit., 198.

16. J. Caringi, op. cit., 172.

17. From a letter addressed to the writer, by Alain Bernaud (June, 1977).

18. B. Tuthill, op. cit., 49.

19. J. G. Marie, quoted in Londeix, op. cit., 228.

20. Rollo Myers, Modern French Music (New York:

21. "Darius Milhaud," in La Revue Musicale, quoted in Hill, op. cit., 370.

22. G. W. Knight, op. cit., 150.

23. G. Wahn, "New Approach Needed by Solo Clarinetists," Woodwind World, Vol. II, No. 1 (Nov., 1957).

24. H. Bruce Lobaugh, "The Clarinet and Its Music in Belgium," The Clarinet, Vol. 3, No. 5 (Fall, 1976) 28.

25. R. Bernard, Histoire de la Musique (Paris: Nathan Edition, Vol. II, 1962), 966.

26. J. Gillespie, The Reed Trio (Detroit: Information Coordinators, Inc., 1971), 53.

27. Huot Fischer, "A Critical Evaluation of Selected Clarinet Solo Literature Published from January 1, 1950 to January 1, 1967" (unpublished D.M.A. dissertation, University of Arizona), 83-84.

28. From a letter addressed to J. Caringi by Ulysse Delécluse, Professor of Clarinet, Conservatoire National Supérieur de Musique (May 2, 1960), op. cit., 171.

29. Claude Rostand, op. cit., 92.

30. H. Kneifer, quoted in Londeix, op. cit.,

31. H. Büsser, "Revue des deux mondes," Press Excerpts.

32. Harry Gee, "Reviews of Recent Clarinet Publications," NACWPI Bulletin, XX, 3 (Spring, 1972), 21.

33. From a letter addressed to the writer, by Christian Manen (May 23, 1977).

34. Norman Heim, "Woodwind Reviews," NACWPI Journal, XXIV, 3 (Spring, 1976), 12.

35. Baker, op. cit., 502.

36. Rostand, op. cit., 116-117.

37. Brymer, op. cit., 222.

38. George Knight, op. cit., 60.

39. Ken Wilson, "New Music Reviews," The Clarinet, Vol. 4, No. 1 (Fall, 1976), 20.

40. Jean Cocteau, quoted in Londeix, op. cit., 88.

41. Letter addressed to the author by Guy Deplus Professor of Clarinet, Conservatoire National Supérieur de Musique (July 14, 1977).

42. J. Brymer, op. cit., 222.

43. Sandra Powell, "I Love Paris in the Springtime," The Clarinet, Vol. 6, No. 2 (Spring, 1979), 24.

44. Letter to the author by Jean Aubain, Director, Conservatoire National de Musique, Versailles (Jan. 24, 1980).

45. Letter to the author by Jean-Paul Holstein (June 16, 1980).

Bibliography

Books

Baker, Theodore. Biographical Dictionary of Musicians. 5th ed., Nicolas Slonimsky. New York: G. Schirmer, 1965.

Bernac, Pierre. Francis Poulenc. Trans. W. Radford. New York: W. W. Norton, 1977.

Bernard, Robert. Histoire de la Musique, Vol. II. Paris: Nathan, 1962.

Brymer, Jack. Clarinet. Ed. Yehudi Menuhin. New York: Macmillan, 1976.

Bull, Storm. Index to Biographies of Contemporary Composers, Vol. II. Metuchen, N. J.: Scarecrow Press, 1974.

Cooper, Martin. French Music. London: Oxford University Press, 1951.

Dumesnil, René. La Musique en France entre les deux Guerres 1919-1939. Paris: Milieu du Monde, 1946.

Dangain, Guy. A propos de la Clarinette. Paris: Gérard Billaudot, 1978.

Die Musik in Geschichte und Gegenwart. Ed. Friedrich Blume. Kassel: Barenreiter-Verlag, 1963.

Errante, Gerard F. A Selective Clarinet Bibliogra-
    phy. Oneonata, N. Y.: Swift-Dorr, 1973.

Ewen, Francois. European Composers Today. New
    York: H. Wilson, 1954.

Gillespie, James E. The Reed Trio: An Annotated
    Bibliography of Original Published Works.
    Detroit: Informational Coordinators, 1971.

Golea, Antoine. Vingt Ans de Musique Contemporaine.
    Paris: Pierre Sehers, 1962.

Grove's Dictionary of Music and Musicians. Ed. Eric
    Blom. London: Macmillan, 1954.

Hill, Edward Burlingame. Modern French Music. New
    York: Houghton Mifflin, 1924.

International Who's Who in Music and Musicians Direc-
    tory. 8th ed., Adrian Gaster. Cambridge: Mel-
    rose Press, 1977.

Kroll, Oskar. The Clarinet. Rev., with Repertory,
    Diethard Riehm; trans. Hilda Morris; ed. Anthony
    Baines. New York: Taplinger, 1968.

Londeix, Jean-Marie. 125 Ans de Musique pour Saxo-
    phone. Paris: Alphonse Leduc, 1971.

Milhaud, Darius. Notes Without Music. New York:
    Knopf, 1953.

Myers, Rollo. Modern French Music. New York:
    Praeger, 1971.

Peyser, Joan. The New Music. New York: Dell, 1971.

Rasmussen, Mary and Donald Mattron. A Teacher's
    Guide to the Literature of Woodwind Instruments.
    Durham: Brass and Woodwind Quarterly, 1966.

Rendall, Geoffrey. The Clarinet. New York: Philo-
    sophical Library, 1954.

Rostand, Claude. French Music Today. Trans. Henry
    Marx. New York: Da Capo Press, 1973.

Slonimsky, Nicolas. Music Since 1900. New York:
    Scribner's, 1971.

Thompson, Oscar. Debussy: Man and Artist. New
    York: Dover, 1967.

Thurston, Frederick. Clarinet Technique. 3rd ed.
    Oxford: Oxford University Press, 1977.

Vinton, John. Dictionary of Contemporary Composers.
    New York: Dutton, 1974.

Voxman, Himmie and Lyle Merriman. Woodwind Solo
    and Study Material. Evanston, Ill.: Instru-
    mentalist, 1975.

Weston, Pamela. Clarinet Virtuosi of the Past.
    London: Robert Hale, 1971.

____. More Clarinet Virtuosi of the Past. London:
    Halstan, 1977.

Whitwell, David. A New History of Wind Music.
    Evanston, Ill.: Instrumentalist, 1972.

Wilkins, Wayne. The Index of Clarinet Music.
    Magnolia, Ark.: Music Register, 1975.

Wolff, Pierre. La Musique Contemporaine. Paris:
    Fernand Nathan, 1954.

Articles

Bonade, Daniel. "Henri Lefebvre," The clarinet, 4
    (Winter, 1950-51), 26-27.

Brody, Clark. "The Debussy Rhapsodie," Woodwind
    World, 3 (April, 1959), 3-4.

Bundy, George F. "Alexandre Selmer as I know Him,"
    Metronome, 48, No. 5 (May, 1932), 28.

Collis, James. "Rabaud's 'Solo de Concours,'" The
    Clarinet, 8 (Winter, 1951-52), 13-19.

Gee, Harry R. "A Survey of Diploma Solos used for

Clarinet at the Paris Conservatory," The
School Musician, 48 (Dec., 1976), 22-23;
(April, 1977), 4-6; 49 (April, 1978), 24-26;
(June, 1978), 19-20; 50 (June-July, 1979), 10-11,

_____. "Gaston Hamelin--Artist and Teacher,"
Bandwagon, 5 (Midwinter, 1957), 8.

_____. "Recent Publications for Clarinet," The
School Musician, 47 (June-July, 1976), 12-13.

_____. "Clarinet Music Reviews," The Clarinet, 5
(Winter, 1978), 24.

_____. "Reviews of Clarinet Publications," The
School Musician, 46 (Feb., 1975), 12-14.

_____. "Style and the Woodwind Performer," Music
Journal, 33 (Nov., 1975), 28-29, 39-40.

_____. "Summer Study in France," The Clarinet, 2
(Dec., 1974), 8-9.

Harman, David. "Jean Xavier Lefèvre, Patriarch of
French Clarinetistry," NACWPI Journal, 23, 4
(Summer, 1975), 22-24.

Heim, Norman. "Reviews of Clarinet Music," NACWPI
Journal, 23, No. 1 (Summer, 1975), 37.

Jennings, Vance S. "The Development of American
Symphonic Clarinet Playing," Woodwind World, 11,
No. 1 (Feb., 1972), 6-8; No. 2 (April, 1972),
6-8.

Lancelot, Jacques. "La Clarinette," Musique et
Radio, 52, No. 619 (Nov., 1962), 27-28.

Maxey, Larry. "The Rose Thirty-two Etudes: A Study
in Metamorphosis," The Clarinet, 1 (Aug., 1974),
8-9.

Merriman, Lyle. "Debussy Premiere Rhapsodie,"
Woodwind World, 6, No. 9 (April, 1966), 4-5.

Mohler, John. "New Music Reviews," The Clarinet, 6,
No. 3 (Spring, 1979), 33.

Pierce, Jerry. "The Bonade Legacy," The Clarinet,
    4, No. 1 (Fall, 1976), 8-9; No. 3 (Spring,
    1977), 14-15; No. 4 (Summer, 1977), 11-12; 6,
    No. 4 (Summer, 1979), 6-13.

Spieler, Ben. "From Paris," Woodwind Magazine, 3
    (March, 1951), 8-13.

Toens, George. "The French School of Clarinetists,"
    Woodwind World, 2, No. 3 (April, 1958), 7-8.

Waln, George E. "Conservatoire National de Paris,"
    The Instrumentalist, 12 (Sept., 1957), 98-100.

_____. "New Approach Needed by Solo Clarinetists,"
    Woodwind World, 1, No. 1 (Nov., 1957), 3.

Weber, David. "Clarinetists of Paris," The Clar-
    inet, 16 (Fall, 1954), 4-7.

Dissertations

Caringi, Joseph. "The Clarinet Contest Solos of
    the Paris Conservatory, with a Performance
    Analysis of Selected Compositions." Unpub-
    lished Ed.D. dissertation, Columbia University,
    1963.

Fischer, Huot. "A Critical Evaluation of Selected
    Clarinet Solo Literature Published from January
    1, 1950 to January 1, 1967." Unpublished D.M.A.
    dissertation, The University of Arizona, 1969.

Knight, George. "A Comparative study of Composi-
    tional Techniques Employed in Instructional
    Materials and Twentieth-Century Solos for the
    Clarinet." Unpublished Ed.D. dissertation,
    University of Illinois, 1973.

Letters to the Author

Arma, Paul. June 9, 1979.

Aubain, Jean. January 24, 1980.

Bibliothèque du Conservatoire de Musique.   July 11,
    1977.

de Blociszewski, J.   February 7, 1980.

Dangain, Guy.   May 6, 1979 and August 3, 1979.

Deplus, Guy.   July 14, 1977 and May 22, 1980.

Gitteau, Claude.   September 1, 1977.

Koechlin, Li.   June 22, 1976.

Selmer, Jean.   June 8, 1979.

Warren, Lester M.   May 25, 1977 and September 29,
    1977.